THE OFFICIAL F1 ITV
FORMULA ONE
1997 GRAND PRIX GUIDE

C000264495

THIS IS A CARLTON BOOK

This edition published in 1997

10 9 8 7 6 5 4 3 2

Text and design copyright ©
Carlton Books Limited 1997

All rights reserved. No part of this
publication may be reproduced, stored
in a retrieval system, or transmitted in
any form or by any means, electronic,
mechanical, photocopying, recording
or otherwise, without the prior
permission of the copyright owner and
the publishers.

A CIP catalogue record for this book is
available from the British Library

ISBN 1 85868 319 X (hardback)
ISBN 1 85868 244 4 (paperback)

Project Editor: Martin Corteel
Project Art Direction: Paul Messam
Production: Sarah Schuman
Design: Steve Wilson
Picture Research: Lorna Ainger and
Brenda Clynch

Printed and bound in Great Britain by
Jarrold Book Printing, Thetford, Norfolk

(Previous page) PRIDE: Formula
One fans show their colours

(Right) GLORY: Schumacher and
Hill soak race-winner Villeneuve
at the 1996 Portuguese GP

(Far right) SPEED: Berger in
action for Benetton

THE OFFICIAL F1ITV

FORMULA ONE
1997 GRAND PRIX GUIDE

Bruce Jones
Editor-at-Large, *Autosport* magazine

CARLTON

CONTENTS

FUTURISTIC: Not Darth Vader, but a French fire marshal

PODIUM PRANKS: Schumacher douses Hill at Imola in 1996

POPPING HIS CORK: Villeneuve celebrates at the Hungaroring

CONGRATULATIONS: Alesi and Schumacher at Estoril

FOREWORD

by Murray Walker

Welcome to Formula One with ITV! 1996 was fast, furious and exciting, right down to that emotional moment when Damon Hill took the chequered flag in Japan to become World Champion, and ITV's first year promises to be just as absorbing. Starting in March new drivers, new cars and new teams will be fighting the established masters tooth and nail for world-wide supremacy. From Australia to Brazil and Hungary to Japan: eight gruelling months ahead and I'm already well and truly fired up to tell you about it, with ITV's new team of experts. Unless I'm very much mistaken, with even fuller coverage, more transmission time and a host of new ideas, the 1997 Grand Prix World Championship is going to make more compelling viewing than ever.

I'm fully aware of the fact that I've got the best job in the world. I'm lucky enough to be able to go to all the races, watch them from the best place, know all the drivers, talk to anyone and be right at the heart of the sport that I love. As a result I have a host of memories, many that are wonderfully enjoyable and some that are tragically sad. James Hunt, Nigel Mansell and Damon Hill winning the World Championships of 1976, 1992 and 1996. The magic and mastery of Niki Lauda, Alain Prost and Ayrton Senna. Dozens of nail-bitingly exciting races. The appalling death of the great Brazilian which brought Formula One to its knees in 1994. I know I'm biased, but for me, with all its highs and lows nothing matches Formula One. Judging from the viewing figures more and more people feel the same way.

If there's one thing I've learned about Grand Prix racing in all these years, though, it is that, to enjoy and appreciate it fully, you need to know as much as you can about its history and personalities. That being so, if you know everything in this book, ITV's first Official Grand Prix Guide, by the time the season starts it is going to give you untold pleasure! Bruce Jones has done a great job of detailing Damon Hill's championship year as well as the teams, the tracks, the drivers and the prospects for 1997. I'll try not to make any mistakes but if I do you'll certainly have the facts to put me right.

Good viewing!

Murray Walker
November 1996

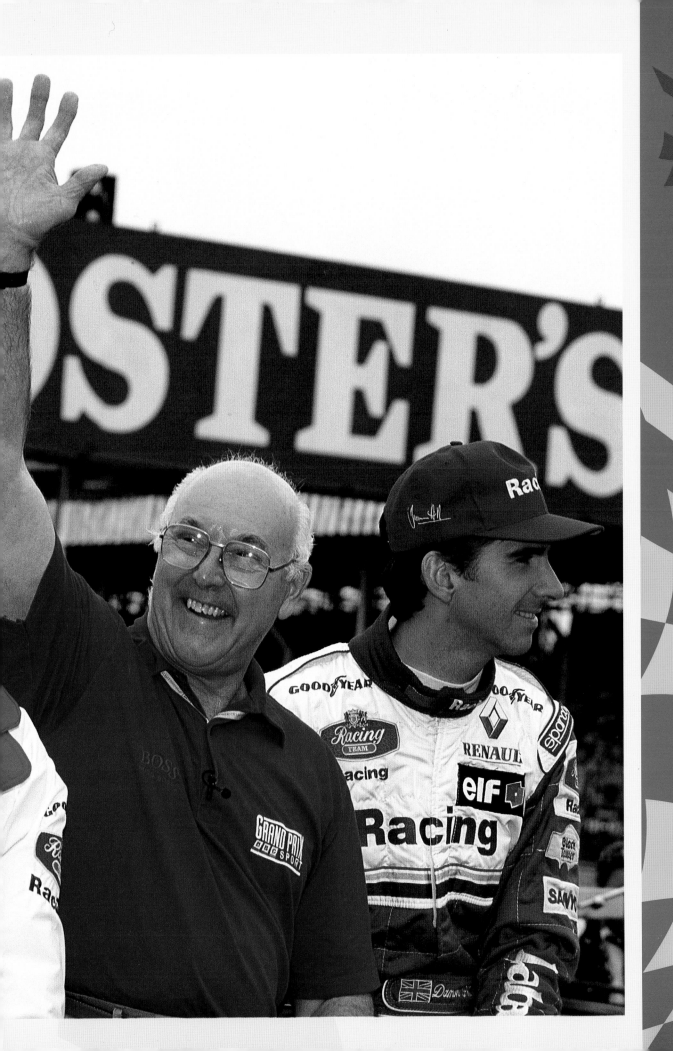

MEDIA FOCUS
Brave new world

fans: Murray Walker. Yes, the ultra-enthusiastic voice of Formula One has moved across from the BBC to scream and shout, but always entertain with his unmatchable enthusiasm.

In on the action
Walker is sharing ITV's commentary booth with recently retired Formula One driver Martin

Formula One has undergone a revolution and you, the TV viewers, are the ones to benefit. For ITV has taken control of the rights to screen the world's most exciting sport, and will bring you Formula One as you've never seen it before. So, strap up tight ... the race is on.

Spreading the gospel of Formula One to a larger slice of the public than ever before was ITV's aim when it took over the contract to screen the Grands Prix in Britain. And even before the engines were fired up for the 1997 season, race fans were able to fuel their cravings for action thanks to ITV's bold new style of coverage. With its new angles, new insights, extra interviews, expert analysis and much more on what goes on behind the scenes, now there's no excuse not to know who is driving for what team and what their chances are.

By talking to the individuals who make the sport tick, such as the team managers, designers and sponsors rather than just to the drivers, ITV gets to the bottom of the story of why any one driver is doing as well, or as badly, as they are. Formula One fanatic Clive James even hosted a special programme on the eve of the first Grand Prix to introduce the cast: the drivers. As the year unfolds, there will be no mysteries, particularly as to what the drivers are really like, both in a racing environment and when they get to relax.

However, there is one constant from Formula One coverage of old for British race

UNDER THE SPOTLIGHT: Media pressure is intense, but drivers must learn to deal with it. Schumacher is on the receiving end here

Brundle who adds his personal knowledge of the contemporary racing scene and his experience as a Formula One driver to Murray's head-on and impassioned delivery.

This duo's excitement is matched by the high-speed activities behind the cameras as the ITV production team choose from pictures from 40 cameras around the track and on the cars, plus slow-motion replays of the key action. ITV is pushing the coverage into the twenty-first century with the use of three-dimensional graphics.

Walker and Co. had plenty to talk about in the season-opening Australian GP, with Brundle's keen eye spotting that Heinz-Harald Frentzen was having brake problems long before they failed and he lost second place. There's no substitute for having been there.

Walker certainly makes up for not having been a racer by leaving no stone unturned in his quest to find out what has been happening. It's not by chance that he knows so much about the Grand Prix world, and his genuine enthusiasm and fair approach opens doors to

him that remain firmly shut for others.

To get to the bottom of the race can often be difficult from the commentary booth, so ITV has employed reporters James Allen and Louise Goodman to rove the pits and the paddock. And the value of this was shown to good effect in Melbourne when Allen was in the Benetton pit area when Jean Alesi repeatedly failed to pit and ran out of fuel.

ITV is taking its own studio to every Grand Prix for expert analysis of events, with veteran anchorman Jim Rosenthal at the helm, joined by Simon Taylor (formerly of Radio 5) and former BBC pit-lane investigator Tony Jardine.

One lap wonders

Coverage of qualifying is one of ITV's trump cards, as qualifying has been transformed in recent years from a hidden part of a Grand Prix weekend to a big part of many fans' enjoyment. If a driver makes a mess in his apportioned hour of truth on the Saturday, he's unlikely to hit gold in the Grand Prix on the following day. Sure, John Watson achieved the amazing feat of winning the United States Grand Prix West at Long Beach in 1983 after starting from 22nd on the grid, but that's very unlikely to happen again. The driver who puts his car on pole position is the one who has the most cause to smile as the cars sit revving on the grid, waiting for the red lights to go out.

ITV is screening a 90-minute programme dedicated to qualifying, so you no longer need to wonder exactly why one of the Ferraris has

RADIO RADIO: Jacques Villeneuve and Damon Hill tackle questions from listeners to a radio programme in one of their many engagements

qualified only 17th. Or, as in the Australian Grand Prix, why Damon Hill's Arrows was so far down the grid.

Lights, noise, action!

All this news and action is expanded upon on

the Sunday in a special half hour slot that introduces the Grand Prix. Then, when all five red starting lights have flicked on in sequence and all gone out, releasing the pent-up horsepower and wall of noise on the rush down the first corner, the race coverage itself

HIGH-SPEED CAMERAS: Jacques Villeneuve took a camera with him wherever he raced in 1996. This was mounted above his head, atop his airbox

BEHIND YOU! Cars in front and cars behind. Race fans at Silverstone are spoiled for choice, surrounded by live action and action replays on massive screen

The other media

It's not all over for Formula One fans when the race is over, as there is always the highlights programme screened later that evening. Then the newspaper reports the following day, usually with follow-up features on the Tuesday. And then, more so in some European countries than elsewhere in the world, there are the weekly magazines such as *Autosport* (in Britain), *Auto Hebdo* (France), *Motor Sport Aktuell* (Germany) and *Autosprint* (Italy) with colour reports, features and all the inside news. The monthly magazines follow, such as *F1 Racing*. Then, at the end of the year, the annuals, the videos, the CD-Roms and the computer games. And, in the past couple of years, web sites have been springing up all over the place as the motorsport information boom continues in all directions. You race fans have never had it so good.

will be underway, with an obvious increase of tempo as Walker changes up through the gears as fast as the drivers themselves. The on-track action will be explained and the likely race tactics discussed as the race unfolds.

The coverage will not stop, as before, after the champagne spraying on the rostrum and a hurried post-race interview. No sir, ITV is offering the experts a chance to give their point-of-view on the events of the day with the advantage of measured consideration and a 20-minute slot. This integral part of the programme is similar to the post-match analysis that has proved so successful in the coverage of other sports such as football, rugby, cricket and even tennis. You want replays of the key moments, you've got them.

And it's not all over then, as there will be a one hour highlights programme screened later in the evening.

Commercial breaks overcome

Being a commercial television station, viewers will be pondering how the advertisement breaks will fit in during race. Well, the ITV programming specialists gave this plenty of thought and have the technology to keep apace with any events that happen during the breaks. They are confident that they will be able to bring you pictures of anything important that happened while you were away, and run it the moment the race returns to your screens. And you can't ask for more than that.

THE ITV TEAM

Murray Walker A Formula One stalwart who needs no introduction. Despite almost half a century covering the sport, he is as wildly enthusiastic as ever, his delivery definitely from the "trousers on fire" school.

Martin Brundle Raced in F1 until the end of 1996 and has 158 Grands Prix to his credit, so he knows what he's talking about.

Jim Rosenthal Long-time ITV front man covering sport right across the board, especially athletics.

Simon Taylor The voice of motor sport on Radio 5, Simon is also head of Haymarket Publishing, which publishes *Autosport*.

Tony Jardine Former employee of Lotus Formula One team before forming his own PR company, Tony has been British TV's man in the pit-lane for the past two years.

James Allen Former journalist who fronted Nigel Mansell's IndyCar TV programme then teamed up with "Our Nige" to ghost his autobiography.

Louise Goodman Stepped out from being PR officer for Jordan Grand Prix. Was a pit reporter for Irish TV in 1996.

REVIEW OF THE 1996 SEASON

The Williams team dominated last year's World Championship and with his eighth win in 16 Grands Prix, Damon Hill was crowned World Champion, just like his father Graham before him. Michael Schumacher, struggling to keep up in his Ferrari, slipped to third

We enter the 1997 Formula One World Championship with a British World Champion in Damon Hill. But this season promises to be very different, as Hill is no longer part of the all-conquering Williams-Renault line-up. Ousted before the year was out, to be replaced by German Heinz-Harald Frentzen, he will be giving his all for the burgeoning TWR Arrows-Yamaha team. Whether he is able to climb to the top of the rostrum remains to be seen. But it was a feat he managed no fewer than eight times in 1996.

Last season was the one in which Hill was going to put the record straight. With Michael Schumacher, World Champion in 1994 and 1995, having moved to Ferrari, there would be no one who could stop the Englishman from emulating his father, the late Graham Hill, by becoming World Champion.

Four wins from the first five Grands Prix gave credence to this ambition, and the Williams team flexed its muscles. But then cruel fate struck, depriving Damon of a clear victory at the Monaco Grand Prix, a race he

has so desperately wanted to win since he arrived in Formula One. On that strange day, just three cars finished, with Olivier Panis a surprise winner for Ligier. Then three spins and retirement in the Spanish Grand Prix also meant no points, and a full-house for Schumacher who put on a masterful display in the wet.

Victories in Canada and France put Hill back on track. But there was no such luck on home ground; in England he fell off and team-mate Jacques Villeneuve took gold.

After a lucky win in Germany when Gerhard Berger's Benetton Renault blew up with three laps to go, Hill had a 21-point lead over Villeneuve, but this was whittled down to 13 after the Belgian Grand Prix as the Canadian picked up momentum. When Hill crashed out of the lead in Italy, matters looked serious, especially when Villeneuve won in Portugal to take the title down to the wire in Japan.

Hill and British racing fans will remember the outcome of that one, as Damon stamped his authority on the proceedings, to sign out in style with a win. However, he was already the first ever second generation World Champion, as Villeneuve had lost a wheel and crashed out 15 laps from the finish. For Hill, this was a life's goal reached at last. For Villeneuve, it was just the beginning.

Apart from this golden duo, Schumacher stood supreme whenever he could coerce his wayward Ferrari to behave; Gerhard Berger and Jean Alesi deserved to win for Benetton, but were consistently deprived; while the McLaren Mercedes pairing of Mika Hakkinen and David Coulthard gave their all and made progress, but are not quite there yet.

At the opposite end of the grid, the Italian Forti team was pitched into oblivion by a financial crisis, leaving Formula One with just 20 cars. However, two more teams are due to join the fray this year, when battle begins again, enlivened by the winter's changes. Hill will find life very different mid-grid, but the Arrows team is sure to make rapid progress.

NOT THIS TIME MICHAEL: Damon Hill points out to outgoing World Champion Michael Schumacher, that it is his turn to be king of Formula One, after clinching the title by winning the Japanese Grand Prix

AUSTRALIAN GP
Jumping Jacques

Debutant Jacques Villeneuve had team-mate Damon Hill beaten. But an oil leak late in the race, scuppered what was set to be one of the most famous victories of all time.

RACE RESULTS

AT ALBERT PARK, MELBOURNE, 10 MARCH 1996

(AFTER 58 LAPS) 1ST ROUND

Pos	Driver	Team
1	DAMON HILL	Williams
2	JACQUES VILLENEUVE	Williams
3	EDDIE IRVINE	Ferrari
4	GERHARD BERGER	Benetton
5	MIKA HAKKINEN	McLaren
6	MIKA SALO	Tyrrell

FASTEST LAP: Jacques Villeneuve 1m 33.421s (127.7mph/205.5km/h)

WEATHER CONDITIONS: Hot, dry and sunny all weekend, 25 °C

Only Mario Andretti and Carlos Reutemann had taken pole position for their debut Grands Prix. But, with seemingly effortless ease, Villeneuve matched the feat of these Formula 1 greats. Granted, the Albert Park circuit in downtown Melbourne was new to everybody, which levelled the playing field, but the French-Canadian IndyCar champion had clearly taken to Formula One and, more importantly, to his Williams-Renault like a natural.

He made a cracking getaway to lead from Hill and Ferrari men Michael Schumacher and Eddie Irvine. Hill made a mistake at the first corner and was back to fourth in a flash. But he would get another shot; the red flags were flying before the lap was over. The race had been stopped.

Brundle goes flying

The reason for the stoppage was one of the most spectacular accidents seen in a Grand Prix for some time. Bunching and swerving in the pack had resulted in Martin Brundle's Jordan colliding with Johnny Herbert's Sauber and David Coulthard's McLaren, before getting airborne and all but splitting in two when it landed. Thanks to the strength of the car's safety cell, Martin climbed out unharmed, was given a medical check-up and then ran for his spare car for the re-start …

Villeneuve has to slow

Villeneuve again got away well and Hill made a better job this time. Indeed, with their order changing only according to pit-stop strategy,

WATCH OUT BEHIND: Benetton's Jean Alesi closes in on Ferrari's Eddie Irvine before running in to him

the Williams duo held down first and second all the way to the flag. But, for the final 20 laps, Hill's car was getting coated with Villeneuve's oil. Clearly, Villeneuve's engine was near to popping, and the team signalled for him to slow. He did so, with good grace, leaving Hill to win as he pleased.

Although Villeneuve slowed, he and Hill were so far clear that he was almost one-and-a-half minutes ahead of Irvine's third placed Ferrari. So, the writing was on the wall: Williams's advantage was even greater than in 1995. The rest would have to catch-up.

BRAZILIAN GP
Hill walks on water

Embarrassed by Villeneuve in Australia, Hill showed who was boss at Williams in Brazil, producing a dominant drive in atrocious conditions for his second win a row.

The biggest surprise after qualifying at Interlagos, was not that Damon Hill had taken pole, but that he had been joined on the front row of the grid by the Peugeot-powered Jordan of local hero Rubens Barrichello. With team-mate Martin Brundle lining up sixth, Eddie Jordan's team was clearly making good the ebullient Irishman's claims that his team would soon be challenging for race wins.

Into a ball of spray

When Hill bogged down in the streaming rain at the start, it seemed that Barrichello may even take the lead, but the Englishman found some precious traction on the treacherous track and propelled his Williams to the head of the spray ball on the run to the first corner, brushing aside a challenge from his own team-mate Jacques Villeneuve.

Making the most of having visibility no other driver was enjoying, Hill pulled away at more than three seconds a lap in the first three laps. The gap stretched at a reduced rate thereafter, but Hill had done enough. The race was won.

The track dried as the race ran its course, but this was no help to Villeneuve, for he spun out of second place when challenged by Jean Alesi's Benetton.

Hill laps Schumacher

Barrichello had fallen to fourth place behind Michael Schumacher's Ferrari during the pit stop sequence, but caught up and enjoyed a fierce tussle, only to spin off as Hill closed up to lap the pair. Such was his domination of the race, that Hill had lapped all bar Alesi by flagfall.

For Schumacher, this was the most chastening moment of his season. Unless Ferrari got its (very expensive) act together, he was going to be eating a lot of humble pie through 1996.

Mika Hakkinen guided his McLaren to points for the second race in a row, showing what a remarkable physical and mental recovery he had made since his life-threatening accident at Adelaide six months earlier. Team-mate David Coulthard was not having such a good time though, and was again neither on the pace nor one of the finishers. It must have seemed a far cry from his days at Williams.

RACE RESULTS
AT INTERLAGOS, SAO PAULO, 31 MARCH 1996

(AFTER 71 LAPS) 2ND ROUND

Pos	Driver	Team
1	DAMON HILL	Williams
2	JEAN ALESI	Benetton
3	MICHAEL SCHUMACHER	Ferrari
4	MIKA HAKKINEN	McLaren
5	MIKA SALO	Tyrrell
6	OLIVIER PANIS	Ligier

FASTEST LAP: Damon Hill 1m 21.547s (118.64mph/190.93km/h)

WEATHER CONDITIONS: Very hot and sunny until heavy rain just before the race, 30 °C

ON THE SIDELINES: Jean Alesi ponders the Williams challenge after spinning off during qualifying

ARGENTINIAN GP
Hill's hat-trick

Leading from lights to flag is what all racing drivers dream of. And this is what Hill did for his third consecutive win, with team-mate Villeneuve the best of the rest.

RACE RESULTS
AT BUENOS AIRES, 7 APRIL 1996
(AFTER 72 LAPS) 3RD ROUND

Pos	Driver	Team
1	DAMON HILL	Williams
2	JACQUES VILLENEUVE	Williams
3	JEAN ALESI	Benetton
4	RUBENS BARRICHELLO	Jordan
5	EDDIE IRVINE	Ferrari
6	JOS VERSTAPPEN	Footwork

FASTEST LAP: Jean Alesi 1m 29.413s (106.55mph/171.48km/h)

WEATHER CONDITIONS: Hot, dry and sunny all weekend, 26 °C

RED-HOT ACTION: Pedro Diniz hastily abandons ship as his Ligier burns after a fuel valve jammed open

Damon Hill had been mighty and victorious when Formula One returned to Argentina in 1995 after a lengthy break. This time he was even mightier and once again victorious. With this victory making it three in a row, Damon said that each one was sweeter than the last. When you're 18 points clear of the nearest challenger after three races of a 16-race campaign, that's hardly surprising.

Hill didn't have it all easy in qualifying though: Michael Schumacher's Ferrari was just a quarter of a second slower.

Hill's perfect start

However, Hill made a perfect start and led away from Schumacher, with Villeneuve making a mess of his clutch and throttle interplay to lose six places. All his hard work in qualifying third had been undone in an instant, as he came round ninth at the end of the lap.

With the Benetton duo of Jean Alesi and Gerhard Berger for company, Hill and Schumacher dropped the pack which had David Coulthard at its head, struggling with his McLaren. However, Villeneuve was making progress and was up to fifth by lap nine, albeit 15 seconds behind Berger.

Schumacher stayed with Hill in the early laps, but he was on a three-stop strategy, so his chances of victory were slim as Hill was faster and planning only two pit visits.

Flaming drama for Diniz

The race was then enlivened by a spectacular accident between Luca Badoer's Forti and Pedro Diniz's Ligier. It appeared Badoer had come off worse as his car flipped, fortunately without injury to the Italian. But, several laps later, after pitting for a new nose cone and fuel, the Brazilian's car was suddenly a fireball. A valve on the fuel nozzle had jammed open and when fuel splashed on to the hot engine, it ignited. Diniz hopped out with minor burns, precipitating a five-lap period when the field circulated behind a safety car.

After the pace car period, the race resumed and almost immediately Schumacher was out, his rear wing mangled by a piece of debris thrown up by Hill's car.

This elevated Alesi to second, but Villeneuve was closing in and made it the second Williams one-two of the year with Alesi the only other driver in contention.

EUROPEAN GP
Villeneuve does it

Victory at only his fourth attempt propelled Jacques Villeneuve into the big time, and added another chapter to the legend started by his late father Gilles, once the king at Ferrari.

When Damon Hill stuck his Williams on pole at the Nurburgring by the huge margin of 0.8 seconds ahead of team-mate Jacques Villeneuve, his rivals could see no result other than a fourth consecutive win for Hill.

Hill blows his start

However, they hadn't reckoned on Hill making an atrocious getaway at the start of the race. And, on a circuit that offers notoriously few overtaking places, he slipped back to fifth behind Villeneuve, David Coulthard (up from sixth), Rubens Barrichello and Michael Schumacher by the first corner.

With Coulthard and Barrichello not as fast as Schumacher and Hill, but able to keep them back, Villeneuve was able to escape. Hill passed Schumacher after six laps, but found it harder to pass Barrichello and was still back in fourth when he decided his car had a handling problem. After pitting for an investigation, Hill rejoined 11th, out of the reckoning.

A flying pitstop for Schumacher elevated him from fourth to second ahead of Coulthard and Barrichello. And so his battle with Villeneuve commenced. Although he caught the Williams by half distance, Germany's hero simply couldn't find a way past.

Villeneuve keeps his cool

One mistake was all it would take for Schumacher to get past and repeat the victory he scored at the same circuit in October 1995. Yet, amazingly, the French-Canadian didn't flinch despite intense pressure and raced on to a fabulous win: the first of many.

Coulthard was delighted with his first rostrum result of the year for McLaren with third, but was over half a minute back. And he had Hill right on his tail when the chequered flag fell, the Williams driver having endured a torrid recovery that included contact with Pedro Diniz's Ligier. While Hill gave his all to overtake Coulthard on the final lap, he had to watch his own tail as Barrichello was ready to pick up any scraps should they tangle, with this trio apart by less than a second.

So, a hiccup for Hill, but he still had an 11 point advantage over Villeneuve.

THE NEW ORDER: Schumacher chased Villeneuve hard, but try as he might, could not find a way past

RACE RESULTS

AT THE NURBURGRING, GERMANY, 28 APRIL 1996

(AFTER 67 LAPS) 4TH ROUND

Pos	Driver	Team
1	JACQUES VILLENEUVE	Williams
2	MICHAEL SCHUMACHER	Ferrari
3	DAVID COULTHARD	McLaren
4	DAMON HILL	Williams
5	RUBENS BARRICHELLO	Jordan
6	MARTIN BRUNDLE	Jordan

FASTEST LAP: Damon Hill 1m 21.363s (125.26mph/201.58km/h)

WEATHER CONDITIONS: Warm and sunny for qualifying, cool and overcast on race day, 12 °C

SAN MARINO GP
Back in control

Damon Hill was back on form in the San Marino Grand Prix at Imola, and blitzed the opposition on Ferrari's home patch for his fourth win of the year.

RACE RESULTS
AT IMOLA, ITALY, 5 MAY 1996
(AFTER 63 LAPS) 5TH ROUND

Pos	Driver	Team
1	DAMON HILL	Williams
2	MICHAEL SCHUMACHER	Ferrari
3	GERHARD BERGER	Benetton
4	EDDIE IRVINE	Ferrari
5	RUBENS BARRICHELLO	Jordan
6	JEAN ALESI	Benetton

FASTEST LAP: Damon Hill 1m 28.931s (123.06mph/198.03km/h)

WEATHER CONDITIONS: Dry and hot for qualifying, dry and warm for race, 22 °C

Damon Hill's misadventures at the Nurburgring were clearly not troubling him at Imola, for he and his Williams were back in control.

Qualifying at Imola traditionally sees a Ferrari setting the pace, whatever the team's contemporary form. People have talked in the past of the cars being run outside the rules on the first day – to pull in the crowds – but that is hearsay, and would not have been needed in 1996. Not with Michael Schumacher behind the wheel of the Prancing Horse's lead car.

Indeed, the German set the crowds baying by edging Hill from pole with a last lap flier.

Coulthard leads the way

However, neither of these two led into the first corner. That honour went to David Coulthard, acknowledged as a master starter. McLaren and Mercedes were delighted to see one of their cars in front for the first time. And the Scottish driver kept it that way until he pitted after 19 laps, with Schumacher and Hill still running in his wake.

While the McLaren and the Ferrari pitted on consecutive laps, the Williams stayed out for a further nine laps, emphasizing its superiority by having stuck with the first pair despite starting the race with a heavier fuel load.

And when he rejoined, Hill was still in the lead, putting to rest the long-held view that the Williams team always failed when it came to clever race tactics.

Indeed, Hill was never troubled for the lead again, with Schumacher given breathing space when Coulthard's hydraulics failed, elevating Gerhard Berger's Benetton to third.

CATCH ME IF YOU CAN: Damon Hill was in sparkling form at Imola, and his two-stop strategy added to his winning margin

Of note was the drive put up by Mika Salo who pushed his Tyrrell up to third position before his first pitstop, rejoined in fourth, only to have his Yamaha engine blow a lap later.

Villeneuve struggles

And what of Jacques Villeneuve, winner of the previous race? After coming round last at the end of the opening lap, he pitted for a puncture to be replaced, having been hit by Jean Alesi at the first corner. Then, after spending the race cleverly working all the way up through the field to sixth place, his suspension broke and he came away with nothing.

MONACO GP
Surprise, surprise!

For Olivier Panis to score his first Grand Prix win at Monaco would have been a fantasy. But to do it in a little-fancied Ligier showed just what a bizarre race this was.

Overtaking in Formula One is tricky at the best of times, but nowhere is like Monaco for cars having to run in line astern. Overtaking? forget it.

So, when French driver Olivier Panis lined up 14th on the grid, victory could not have been further from his mind. Yet, he hit the front on lap 60 and was still leading when the chequered flag fell 15 laps later, with just three cars still running. So, what happened?

Cruel luck for Hill

Damon Hill blasted past pole-sitter Michael Schumacher on the run to the first corner. And, once in front, the Williams driver powered away until his engine blew, meaning he had to wait a year to make another bid to win the Grand Prix his late father, Graham, won five times.

Schumacher was not so impressive, crashing out on the opening lap, caught out by the wet conditions. With Hill gone, Jean Alesi took over. But, he also had to retire when his Benetton's suspension collapsed, leaving Panis in front after accidents had accounted for Martin Brundle, Ricardo Rosset, Ukyo Katayama, Jos Verstappen and Rubens Barrichello, plus the self-eliminating Minardi drivers Pedro Lamy and Giancarlo Fisichella.

Panis hits the front

However, this was no fluke, for Panis had been lapping faster than everyone except Alesi as the track dried out. And, he overtook people. For the final laps, he was pushed hard by David Coulthard's McLaren. But if you want to make your car "wide" there's no place like Monaco, and Panis was able to secure his first win, which was also his team's first for 15 years. The joy, as one would expect, was unconfined.

Coulthard backed off to be sure of securing second, and he had room to do so, because Johnny Herbert was some way back in third.

Fourth place looked set to go to Mika Salo, but he was being pressed hard by compatriot Mika Hakkinen when they came upon Eddie Irvine's spun (and twice lapped) Ferrari and they were unable to avoid it. This promoted Herbert's Sauber team-mate Heinz-Harald Frentzen, but he couldn't even be bothered to cross the line at the finish, reporting to the pits instead. It was, indeed, a most unusual two hours.

RACE RESULTS
AT MONACO, 19 MAY 1996
(AFTER 75 LAPS) 6TH ROUND

Pos	Driver	Team
1	OLIVIER PANIS	Ligier
2	DAVID COULTHARD	McLaren
3	JOHNNY HERBERT	Sauber
4	HEINZ H. FRENTZEN	Sauber
5	MIKA SALO	Tyrrell
6	MIKA HAKKINEN	McLaren

FASTEST LAP: Jean Alesi 1m 25.205s (87.37mph/140.61km/h)

WEATHER CONDITIONS: Cloudy for qualifying, rain before the race, drizzle towards the end, 11 °C

BOLT FROM THE BLUE: Olivier Panis's win for Ligier was the biggest turn up for the books in years

SPANISH GP
Rain man

Stamped with the mark of genius, this was one of those drives that comes along only occasionally as Michael Schumacher destroyed the opposition in the rain, in Spain.

RACE RESULTS

AT BARCELONA, 2 JUNE 1996

(AFTER 65 LAPS) 7TH ROUND

Pos	Driver	Team
1	MICHAEL SCHUMACHER	Ferrari
2	JEAN ALESI	Benetton
3	JACQUES VILLENEUVE	Williams
4	HEINZ H. FRENTZEN	Sauber
5	MIKA HAKKINEN	McLaren
6	PEDRO DINIZ	Ligier

FASTEST LAP: Michael Schumacher
WEATHER CONDITIONS: Torrential rain

The rain in Spain falls mainly, it seems, on Barcelona… It may have been June, but the temperature was in low single figures, the crowd was soaked and there hadn't been much of a race to watch. But, strangely, no one cared, for this was one of the great drives of modern motor racing history.

On a track awash with puddles, and rain teeming from the leaden sky, Schumacher had performed miracles. And frankly, made every other driver seem merely mortal, just members of his supporting cast.

Schumacher slips up

Third on the grid in his Ferrari behind the two Williams drivers, the German made an atrocious getaway and fell to ninth place. However, he was up to sixth when they came round to complete the opening lap.

Blinded by spray, the reigning World Champion could have been excused for hanging back and driving with a little caution in the early going. But he, and he alone, was not interested in this.

Team-mate Eddie Irvine spun out terminally on lap two and yielded fifth.

Hill spins

Then Damon Hill rotated away his place three laps later and Gerhard Berger was passed by the end of lap five. Only Jean Alesi and Jacques Villeneuve to go, and they were passed on laps 9 and 12 respectively, both losing out at the tight La Caixa left-hander.

Schumacher then simply drove off into the distance, pulling away by as much as four seconds per lap, which didn't brighten the afternoon's proceedings for those in the

WET-WEATHER WONDER: Michael Schumacher drives inside Jean Alesi en route to a mighty victory

grandstands. But it was a truly masterful display of car control in conditions that caught out six cars before two laps were completed.

Hill had a poor day, spinning twice before a third spin saw him park his car against the pit wall. Johnny Herbert, Gerhard Berger and Jos Verstappen also crashed out.

Alesi, troubled by a car set so low it was aquaplaning regularly, limped home second, with Villeneuve close behind in third. With Rubens Barrichello's clutch having blown, Heinz-Harald Frentzen took fourth. This was a fine reward as he had endured a huge shunt in the morning warm-up. Mika Hakkinen was fifth and Pedro Diniz claimed his first point in sixth.

CANADIAN GP
Flags fly for Jacques

Romantics wanted French-Canadian Jacques Villeneuve to romp to victory on the circuit named after his father. But team-mate Damon Hill was not in a romantic mood.

Many seasoned visitors to the Canadian Grand Prix had never seen the flag of Quebec before, just the regular red and white maple leaf of Canada. But this time it was different, for the French-Canadian population of Montreal was out in force, with one of its own to cheer on: Jacques Villeneuve. And he's not just any old son of the region: he's son of Canada's greatest ever driver, after whom the Circuit Gilles Villeneuve is named.

Feted wherever he went, Villeneuve found solace only when he was alone in the cockpit. And he did well, only being pipped to pole by 0.02 seconds by Damon Hill.

Ferrari's failure

With Michael Schumacher qualifying his Ferrari close to the Williams pair, it was important that both got off the line smartly.

This they did, but they needn't have worried, for Schumacher failed to get his engine to fire at the start of the parade lap and had to start from the rear of the grid. Then, despite tearing through the field, he retired with driveshaft failure. With team-mate Eddie Irvine dropping out after a lap with a suspension wishbone fault, it was a wretched day for Ferrari.

Untroubled by the Ferraris, Damon Hill led away from Jacques Villeneuve and Jean Alesi. And Hill pulled away at a noticeable rate, suggesting that he had started with less fuel on board than his rivals. Indeed, this proved to be the case, for Hill stopped twice to Villeneuve's one stop, but the tactic was correct – albeit only by a fraction – he rejoined after his second stop just in front and was able to notch up his fifth win of the year. This stretched his points advantage to 21.

RACE RESULTS

AT CIRCUIT GILLES VILLENEUVE, MONTREAL, 16 JUNE 1996

(AFTER 69 LAPS) 8TH ROUND

Pos	Driver	Team
1	DAMON HILL	Williams
2	JACQUES VILLENEUVE	Williams
3	JEAN ALESI	Benetton
4	DAVID COULTHARD	McLaren
5	MIKA HAKKINEN	McLaren
6	MARTIN BRUNDLE	Jordan

FASTEST LAP: Jacques Villeneuve
 1m 21.916s (120.75mph/194.33km/h)
**WEATHER CONDITIONS: Warm, dry
 and bright in qualifying, cooler for
 the race, 24 °C**

Brundle thwarted

Alesi's Benetton was never really in touch, yet resisted team-mate Gerhard Berger until the Austrian spun out and Martin Brundle clashed with Pedro Lamy's Minardi and had to pit, allowing the two McLaren men David Coulthard and Mika Hakkinen through.

WILLIAMS TO THE FORE: Hill leads away from Villeneuve and Alesi, while Schumacher is right at the back

FRENCH GP
A gift for Damon

Christmas came early for Damon Hill when Michael Schumacher's pole-sitting Ferrari blew up on the parade lap. And it was left to the Englishman to cruise to his sixth win.

RACE RESULTS
AT MAGNY-COURS, 30 JUNE 1996

(AFTER 72 LAPS) 9TH ROUND

Pos	Driver	Team
1	DAMON HILL	Williams
2	JACQUES VILLENEUVE	Williams
3	JEAN ALESI	Benetton
4	GERHARD BERGER	Benetton
5	MIKA HAKKINEN	McLaren
6	DAVID COULTHARD	McLaren

FASTEST LAP: Jacques Villeneuve 1m 18.610s (120.89mph/194.55km/h)

WEATHER CONDITIONS: Hot, dry and sunny all weekend, 26 °C

Damon Hill arrived in France with his head held high. Renault had announced they would be pulling out of Formula One at the end of 1997, but Hill would give them not only the home win they wanted, but also the World Championship so they could carry the prestigious number one in their final season. Fresh from victory in Canada, there was every reason to believe that victory at Magny-Cours would be a formality.

Pipped for pole

But then Michael Schumacher stuck his Ferrari on pole after a dramatic qualifying session that saw no fewer than five drivers swap pole on nine occasions. Hill would start second, with the Benettons of Jean Alesi and Gerhard Berger next

up, ahead of Mika Hakkinen's McLaren. Hill's team-mate Villeneuve would start the line up, but he was fortunate to start at all after enduring a 130mph impact at the Estoril corner.

The race was turned on its head halfway around the final parade lap. A puff of smoke from the rear of the lead car turned into a full-blooded billow and Schumacher parked up. His race was over before it had started.

Thus Hill made the most of what was effectively pole position, with a great start to break the tow to the pack behind. Suitably unencumbered by attacks from Alesi, he ran his own race, only relinquishing the lead when making the first of his two pitstops. Basically, for Hill, the race went like clockwork.

OVER AND OUT: Michael Schumacher's Ferrari is carried away after failing on the parade lap

Clouds over Ferrari

Both Ferraris had failed in the previous race, so a dark cloud descended on the team when Irvine stopped five laps into the race. Having chased Alesi and Hakkinen for the first half of the race, Villeneuve atoned for his car-wrecking shunt by climbing to second and staying there to flagfall, even closing on Hill. While Alesi had to dig deep to hold off team-mate Berger for third. Completing the two-by-two pattern, Hakkinen headed home team-mate Coulthard.

BRITISH GP
Villeneuve strikes back

RACE RESULTS
AT SILVERSTONE, 14 JULY 1996
(AFTER 61 LAPS) 10TH ROUND

Pos	Driver	Team
1	JACQUES VILLENEUVE	Williams
2	GERHARD BERGER	Benetton
3	MIKA HAKKINEN	McLaren
4	RUBENS BARRICHELLO	Jordan
5	DAVID COULTHARD	McLaren
6	MARTIN BRUNDLE	Jordan

FASTEST LAP: Jacques Villeneuve
1m 29.288s (127.09mph/204.53km/h)
WEATHER CONDITIONS: Warm, dry
and sunny, except when cloudy in
warm-up, 22 °C

Damon Hill desperately wanted to win at home. He claimed pole, but blew his start, and this was just what his Williams team-mate Jacques Villeneuve wanted for his second win.

Starting on pole position ought to mean you reach the first corner in the lead. But, after a wretched getaway, Hill filtered into Copse corner with his Williams back in fifth place. In the batting of an eyelid, he had dropped behind Jacques Villeneuve, Jean Alesi, Mika Hakkinen and Michael Schumacher. He had to make up places, and make them up fast, because Villeneuve was starting to break clear.

More Ferrari failure

While Villeneuve edged clear, Hill's chase was made easier when Schumacher's Ferrari continued its mechanical nightmare and pulled off on the third lap. Then, sure enough, team-mate Eddie Irvine lasted just two laps longer. If Ferrari had been a French team, a guillotine would have been erected.

Hakkinen was Hill's next target. Hill edged closer and was hot on the Finn's heels shortly after his first scheduled pitstop. Catching him was one thing; passing was another. But a loose wheel pitched Hill deep into the Copse gravel trap and retirement. With their hero out, the partisan British crowd packed their coolboxes and headed home.

Loose wheel blues

Villeneuve kept going in exemplary style with Hakkinen rising to second place, albeit half-a-minute behind when Benetton men Jean Alesi and Gerhard Berger pitted for the first and only time. But Alesi was not to finish – a wheel bearing had failed – he was out a lap after Berger had demoted the slowing Frenchman. A lap later, the Austrian was up to second, overhauling Hakkinen when the Finn made his second stop at the pits.

And that was it, in the dreariest race of the season, with Jacques Villeneuve winning by almost 20 seconds from Gerhard Berger. In a year of racing on circuits he'd not seen before the race weekend, the little French-Canadian pointed out that all the pre-season testing the team had done at Silverstone had made all the difference. And, of course, Hill's poor start.

Mika Hakkinen managed to claim the final place on the rostrum, ahead of the Jordans of Rubens Barrichello and the lapped Martin Brundle, both of whom sandwiched David Coulthard in his McLaren.

ROUGH RIDER: Damon Hill crashes out of third place due to a loose wheel

GERMAN GP
Berger's bad luck

This should have been Gerhard Berger's race. But a puff of smoke signalled failure for the Austrian Benetton driver, and victory for the closely following Damon Hill.

Gerhard Berger had been consistently getting closer to the pace in recent races. And his second place at Silverstone was followed by second place on the grid at Hockenheim, behind only Damon Hill, a driver who was racing amid rumours that he was to be dumped by Williams at the end of the year.

Amazingly, Hill made another weak start and the Austrian pushed his Benetton into the lead, followed by team-mate Jean Alesi who rocketed up from fifth to head Hill into the first corner. Fortunately, Hill could concentrate on pressuring the Frenchman, as Michael Schumacher, David Coulthard and Jacques Villeneuve were falling away behind him.

Poor Williams tactics

Clearly bottled up behind Alesi, Hill ought to have been brought in for his first pitstop early, but the team kept him out until long after others had stopped. But not the Benettons, which were on a one-stop strategy. Four laps after he pitted, Hill hit the front, but only after the Benettons came in. The trouble was, he was due one more stop and they were set for the run to the flag.

Catching is one thing . . .

Despite opening out his advantage over Berger to 16 seconds before he pitted again, Hill was two seconds behind on rejoining and faced with chasing the faster of the two Benettons over the remaining 11 laps. It took just three to catch Berger, but after a further five, he'd found no chinks in his armour.

But then a puff of smoke turned to a billow and a disconsolate Berger rolled to a halt, his engine blown, giving Hill an easy win.

Behind them, Alesi was safe in second, with Villeneuve having worked his way up to third, surviving a near collision in the pits when Schumacher swerved in front of him, before going away for good.

And so the thousands of Schumacher fans had to make do with cheering their hero as he resisted Coulthard for fourth.

RACE RESULTS
AT HOCKENHEIM, 28 JULY 1996
(AFTER 45 LAPS) 11TH ROUND

Pos	Driver	Team
1	DAMON HILL	Williams
2	JEAN ALESI	Benetton
3	JACQUES VILLENEUVE	Williams
4	MICHAEL SCHUMACHER	Ferrari
5	DAVID COULTHARD	McLaren
6	RUBENS BARRICHELLO	Jordan

FASTEST LAP: Damon Hill 1m 46.504s (143.31mph/230.63km/h)

WEATHER CONDITIONS: Hot, dry and sunny all weekend, overcast for race, 28 °C

BENETTON TO THE FORE: Gerhard Berger leads team-mate Jean Alesi and Damon Hill into the first corner. Hill would spend the race in pursuit

HUNGARIAN GP
The battle is on

Victory in Hungary would have put Damon Hill on course for the Formula One title. But Williams team-mate Jacques Villeneuve had other ideas and kept him at bay to the finish.

RACE RESULTS

AT THE HUNGARORING, 11 AUGUST 1996

(AFTER 77 LAPS) 12TH ROUND

Pos	Driver	Team
1	JACQUES VILLENEUVE	Williams
2	DAMON HILL	Williams
3	JEAN ALESI	Benetton
4	MIKA HAKKINEN	McLaren
5	OLIVIER PANIS	Ligier
6	RUBENS BARRICHELLO	Jordan

FASTEST LAP: Damon Hill 1m 20.093s (110.85mph/178.38km/h)

WEATHER CONDITIONS: Hot, dry and sunny all weekend, 28 °C

RELEASE OF PRESSURE: Jaques Villeneuve unleashes the bubbly after resisting Damon Hill to the end

emerging ahead of Alesi. Job done? Not quite – Hill was delayed by two backmarkers – Alesi dived past before he had time to get his tyres up to operating temperature. However, five laps later Alesi ran wide and Hill was through into third place and off after Schumacher.

One stop too many

Sadly for Hill, Williams had put him on to a three-stop strategy and this would make it almost impossible for him to win, however hard he drove on the run to the chequered flag.

Hill caught Schumacher, but could not pass. Then Schumacher pitted and Hill elected to stay out a while longer to open up a big enough gap so he would be able to rejoin the race in second place after his third stop. And this is exactly what happened.

Villeneuve was given a scare just before Hill's third stop when the Canadian made his second, as a wheelnut crossthreaded and time was lost. He had just 6.5 seconds in hand when he rejoined and Hill was charging. Down and down came the gap, but Villeneuve hung on, by 0.77 seconds for his third win.

Third place went to Alesi, benefiting when, seven laps from home, Schumacher's throttle packed up. Alesi should also have finished behind team-mate Gerhard Berger, but the Austrian driver's Renault engine failed for the second race in a row.

Nowhere has two sides of the track that are so different as the Hungaroring. Sit on the left-hand side of the main straight, on the racing line, and the track is clean. But the side by the pit wall is untouched by a tyre until the grid assembles for the race. And, as a consequence, it's as dusty as hell.

Lost in the dust

So, when Damon Hill, who'd qualified second to Michael Schumacher, attempted to put the power down at the start of the race, he accelerated with even less alacrity than usual.

In an instant, Hill was down in fourth, facing the prospect of a long afternoon; he was trapped behind Jean Alesi, just as he had been at the German Grand Prix.

Schumacher set a fair pace ahead of Jacques Villeneuve as they pulled clear, but it was nothing that Hill couldn't have matched had he passed Alesi. The problem was, the Hungaroring is too twisty and narrow for overtaking.

Schumacher lost out to Villeneuve when they made their first pitstops, with Hill also

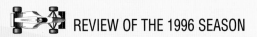

BELGIAN GP
Schumacher's favour

Michael Schumacher has done Damon Hill very few favours over the years, but by beating Jacques Villeneuve to victory in Belgium, he stopped Hill's points advantage from being slashed.

RACE RESULTS

AT SPA-FRANCORCHAMPS,
25 AUGUST 1996

(AFTER 44 LAPS) 13TH ROUND

Pos	Driver	Team
1	MICHAEL SCHUMACHER	Ferrari
2	JACQUES VILLENEUVE	Williams
3	MIKA HAKKINEN	McLaren
4	JEAN ALESI	Benetton
5	DAMON HILL	Williams
6	GERHARD BERGER	Benetton

FASTEST LAP: Gerhard Berger
1m 53.067s (137.87mph/221.87km/h)
WEATHER CONDITIONS: Warm and sunny, except light rain in qualifying, 24 °C

WHAT COULD HAVE BEEN: McLaren men Coulthard and Hakkinen head the field; but not for very long

Damon Hill's inability to get off the grid quickly was a factor in the second half of 1996. Second on the grid at Spa-Francorchamps, it struck again, and Hill was third into the first corner behind Jacques Villeneuve and Michael Schumacher. Then, two corners later, he was demoted further by David Coulthard's McLaren.

Still, at least Hill was in a better position than that enjoyed by Sauber's Heinz-Harald Frentzen and Ligier's Johnny Herbert and Olivier Panis. Rubens Barrichello was also involved, but limped back to the pits.

Verstappen causes chaos

Villeneuve and Schumacher edged clear, only to have their advantage negated when Jos Verstappen had a huge shunt at Stavelot in his Footwork and brought out the safety car, which bunched the field while the debris was cleared. Many took the opportunity to make their first pitstop. Trouble was, Villeneuve misheard his crew and stayed out an extra lap, coming in when Hill expected to pit. Not only did this let Schumacher get ahead, but it forced Hill to trickle through the pit entry road and back on to the track, which left him 13th when he rejoined after pitting at the end of the following lap.

McLaren hits the front

When the pace car pulled off, Coulthard led from McLaren team-mate Mika Hakkinen, to the delight of the team and its engine supplier Mercedes. Trouble was, neither had yet pitted and they duly dropped down the order.

When Villeneuve pitted two laps later than Schumacher for their second stop, it looked as though the Canadian had done the trick, for he rejoined in the lead, cutting across Schumacher's bows. But Schumacher jinked to his inside and was ahead before Villeneuve could get the power down …

And that was how it stayed, with the Ferrari pulling clear in the closing laps. With Hill managing to climb back only as high as fifth behind Hakkinen and Jean Alesi, his advantage was cut back by four points. But, had Schumacher not driven so well, the deficit could have come down by eight.

ITALIAN GP
Ferrari's home win

One slip was all it took for Damon Hill to throw away a title-clinching win. And who should be there to pick up the pieces but Ferrari's own Michael Schumacher.

They may have looked tame when they were fixed behind the kerbs at the apex of the chicanes. Indeed, they had actually been requested by the drivers themselves after Jacques Villeneuve's Williams had been hit by a lump of concrete thrown up when another car crossed the kerbs ahead of him. However, Monza's tyre stacks will long be talked about as the bane of the 1996 Italian Grand Prix.

For once, Damon Hill made a good start and led Villeneuve on the run to the first corner. So, advantage Hill. Indeed, with his 13-point advantage a win would wrap up the title. But, amazingly, Alesi nosed his Benetton into the lead, up from sixth on the grid.

Hill breaks clear

Hill was back ahead before the lap was out, though. Better still, as far as he was concerned, Villeneuve had been demoted to fourth by Mika Hakkinen, while Michael Schumacher had fallen from third to sixth.

On lap two, Villeneuve grazed a tyre stack and bent his front suspension. Then some tyres sprang back into Coulthard's path and he was out on the spot. Six laps in, and under no pressure as he pulled clear, Hill clipped a tyre stack and terminally bent his suspension. Heinz-Harald Frentzen, now confirmed as Hill's replacement at Williams for 1997, Ricardo Rosset and Eddie Irvine were also claimed by the tyre stacks, while Hakkinen got away with a pitstop for a new nosewing after Alesi flicked tyres into his path.

Ferrari's glory

This laid the way clear for Schumacher to chase Alesi. But the Benetton stayed in front, until the first pitstop. The cheer was almost as deafening as the cars when the Ferrari emerged in the lead. But that was nothing compared to the cheer that went up as Schumacher took the chequered flag for Ferrari's first home win since 1988.

Gerhard Berger's bad luck struck again and he retired after only four laps. This allowed Hakkinen to climb back to third, clear of the nose-to-tail Jordans of Martin Brundle and Rubens Barrichello.

With his car's handling awry, Villeneuve kept going, but he couldn't quite score, as Pedro Diniz claimed the final point ahead of him. Hill had failed to clinch the title at Monza, but his points advantage remained intact.

BRAVO, BRAVO:
Michael Schumacher
sent the *tifosi* delirious
by winning for Ferrari

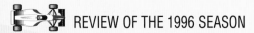

PORTUGUESE GP
Around the outside

A stunning victory for Jacques Villeneuve was more than demoralizing for Damon Hill. For it also meant that the World Championship would go all the way to the final round.

RACE RESULTS

AT ESTORIL, 22 SEPTEMBER 1996

(AFTER 70 LAPS) 15TH ROUND

Pos	Driver	Team
1	JACQUES VILLENEUVE	Williams
2	DAMON HILL	Williams
3	MICHAEL SCHUMACHER	Ferrari
4	JEAN ALESI	Benetton
5	EDDIE IRVINE	Ferrari
6	GERHARD BERGER	Benetton

FASTEST LAP: Jacques Villeneuve 1m 22.873s (117.68mph/189.38km/h)

WEATHER CONDITIONS: Warm, dry and sunny all weekend, 24 °C

No one overtakes around the outside at Estoril's 180-degree final corner. It's just not done. Everybody knows that, except Jacques Villeneuve. When he told his crew that he reckoned it would be possible, they told him they would not enjoy scraping him from the barriers. But, showing refreshing initiative, to say nothing of sheer feistiness, he not only tried this move in the race, but used it to pass none other than Michael Schumacher.

Move of the year

And the moment was a crucial one, for he had been bottled up behind Schumacher after a poor start from second on the grid, as Damon Hill and Jean Alesi escaped up the road.

On lap 15, they came across the Minardi of backmarker Giovanni Lavaggi and Schumacher was marginally delayed on the entry to the final corner. Not waiting for another chance, Villeneuve went for the outside line. Shocked by the move, Schumacher had to run the risk

of their wheels touching with unimaginably dire consequences before the move was complete. It rocked all who saw it.

Once past Schumacher, Villeneuve set off after Jean Alesi, but Hill was pulling clear of the Benetton driver with every lap, and appeared to be cruising to the world title.

Then it became clear that he was not dropping Villeneuve. In fact, his young team-mate was catching him. Villeneuve moved up to second after the first batch of pitstops, and though he was some 15 seconds down, he was still lapping faster. Then Hill was thwarted to the tune of four seconds on one lap as he got caught among backmarkers. When Hill came in for his second pitstop that gap was down to just 5 seconds. Several laps later, Villeneuve was on to Hill's tail. In for the final stop, Hill was ahead. But when Villeneuve came out a lap later, it was he who was in the lead. And Villeneuve motored clear to win by 20 seconds as Hill was afflicted with a clutch problem.

McLAREN AT WAR: Mika Hakkinen bounds over the chicane kerbs to pitch team-mate David Coulthard into a spin

Schumacher claimed a distant third place, with Alesi fourth, before another huge gap back to Eddie Irvine who survived an attack by Gerhard Berger at the last corner on the final lap. However, even having spun, he was still able to beat the Austrian to the line.

McLarens at war

This wasn't the only contact, as the McLaren duo of Mika Hakkinen and David Coulthard became involved in their own warfare after the Finn ran into the back of the Scot at the unpopular uphill chicane. Coulthard was pitched into a spin, pitted for a check-over, came in again for a slow puncture to be replaced, and then was called in one more time for a stop-go penalty for speeding in the pits. He was to be classified 13th.

JAPANESE GP
Job done!

Thousands of British fans were bleary-eyed when they ate their breakfast on Sunday, October 13, as they'd got out of their beds before dawn to watch Damon Hill crowned World Champion.

The years of blood, sweat and tears were all worth it, many times over, for Damon Hill when he wrapped up the World Championship in Japan. In so doing, he became the first to complete a father-and-son double, emulating the feat his late father Graham managed in 1962 and 1968. To make the long close-season before he joins TWR Arrows all the sweeter, Damon rounded off his season with a win.

Coming to Suzuka, Hill was nine points clear of Villeneuve. With 10 points for a win, his team-mate could overhaul him. But to ensure the title was his, all Hill had to do was claim the point for sixth. His rivals reckoned anyone could do that in a Williams. But no one would deny that fate may conspire against Hill.

Dream start for Hill

However, come the day, it was Villeneuve who was to be hit with bad luck. On pole ahead of Hill, he fluffed his start and was sixth as they funnelled into the first corner. And Hill was first, with the race under control, lapping fast enough to stay out front, but doing everything he could to save his car from breaking down.

The Benetton drivers seemed to have something in for Williams that day – Jean Alesi just missed Villeneuve during his sizeable shunt on the opening lap. Then, two laps later, Berger made an optimistic dive to pass Hill into the final chicane and nearly took him off. But, to the relief of all the early-risers in Britain, Hill escaped and was never troubled again.

Villeneuve crashes out

With 15 laps to go, the championship was Hill's. Villeneuve had his right rear wheel part company with the car shortly after his second pitstop, crashing out. Hill tried not to let it affect his concentration, but the realization that he was champion, even if he retired, must have

been ultra-emotional. However, hold on he did, crossing the line for his 21st win, and perhaps last for a while, as he brought his career at the pace-setting Williams team to a close.

Michael Schumacher and Mika Hakkinen were not far behind as Hill slowed and zapped his team as he passed the chequer, while Berger pitted early for a new nose after his move on Hill and still made it up to fourth despite tangling with Eddie Irvine for the second race in a row.

Martin Brundle claimed fifth for Jordan, with Heinz-Harald Frentzen taking the final point for Sauber. He will be hoping for rather bigger rewards when he is driving for Williams in 1997.

When it was all over, the drivers and their teams headed for Suzuka's famed venue, the Log Cabin. Renowned for its sky-high drink prices and end-of-term japes. And, as of 1996, for head shaving: when Damon took to the karaoke machine, he had a set of backing singers who looked remarkably like bald-headed versions of Villeneuve, Salo and Coulthard. Which, indeed, they were.

It should have grown back by Melbourne.

RACE RESULTS

AT SUZUKA, 13 OCTOBER 1996

(AFTER 52 LAPS) 16TH ROUND

Pos	Driver	Team
1	DAMON HILL	Williams
2	MICHAEL SCHUMACHER	Ferrari
3	MIKA HAKKINEN	McLaren
4	GERHARD BERGER	Benetton
5	MARTIN BRUNDLE	Jordan
6	HEINZ H. FRENTZEN	Sauber

FASTEST LAP: Jacques Villeneuve 1m 44.043s (126.09mph/202.92km/h)

WEATHER CONDITIONS: Warm, dry and sunny on race day, damp in qualifying, 22 °C

CHANGING THE GUARD: Outgoing champion Michael Schumacher helps Damon Hill celebrate his 1996 title

1996 Drivers' Championship

POS	DRIVER	(NAT)	CAR	Australian GP	Brazilian GP	Argentinian GP	European GP	San Marino GP	Monaco GP	Spanish GP	Canadian GP	French GP	British GP	German GP	Hungarian GP	Belgian GP	Italian GP	Portuguese GP	Japanese GP	PTS
1	Damon Hill	(GBR)	Williams-Renault FW18	1	1♦*	1♦	4♦*	1*	■	■♦	1♦	1	■♦	1♦*	2*	5	■♦	2♦	1	97
2	Jacques Villeneuve	(CAN)	Williams-Renault FW18	2♦*	■	2	1	11	■	3	2*	2*	1*	3	1	2♦	7	1*	■♦*	78
3	Michael Schumacher	(GER)	Ferrari F310	■	3	■	2	2♦	■♦	1*	■	▲♦	■	4	■♦	1	1*	3	2	59
4	Jean Alesi	(FRA)	Benetton-Renault B196	■	2	3*	■	6	■*	2	3	3	■	2	3	4	2	4	■	47
5	Mika Hakkinen	(FIN)	McLaren-Mercedes MP4/11	5	4	■	8	8	6	5	5	5	3	■	4	3	3	■	3	31
6	Gerhard Berger	(AUT)	Benetton-Renault B196	4	■	■	9	3	■	■	■	4	2	■	■	6*	■	6	4	21
7	David Coulthard	(GBR)	McLaren-Mercedes MP4/11	■	■	7	3	■	2	■	4	6	5	5	■	■	■	13	8	18
8	Rubens Barrichello	(BRA)	Jordan-Peugeot 196	■	■	4	5	5	■	■	■	9	4	6	6	■	5	■	9	14
9	Olivier Panis	(FRA)	Ligier-Mugen JS43	7	6	8	■	■	1	■	■	7	■	7	5	■	■	10	7	13
10	Eddie Irvine	(GBR)	Ferrari F310	3	7	5	■	4	■	■	■	■	■	■	■	■	■	5	■	11
11	Martin Brundle	(GBR)	Jordan-Peugeot 196	■	■	■	6	■	■	■	6	8	6	10	■	■	4	9	5	8
12	Heinz-Harald Frentzen	(GER)	Sauber-Ford C15	8	■	■	■	■	4	4	■	■	8	8	■	■	■	7	6	7
13	Mika Salo	(FIN)	Tyrrell-Yamaha 024	6	5	■	●	■	5	■	■	10	7	9	■	7	■	11	■	5
14	Johnny Herbert	(GBR)	Sauber-Ford C15	▲	■	9	7	■	3	■	7	●	9	■	■	■	9	8	10	4
15	Pedro Diniz	(BRA)	Ligier-Mugen JS43	10	8	■	10	7	■	6	■	■	■	■	■	■	6	■	■	2
16	Jos Verstappen	(NLD)	Footwork-Hart FA17	■	■	6	■	■	■	■	■	■	■	10	■	■	8	■	11	1
	Ukyo Katayama	(JAP)	Tyrrell-Yamaha 024	11	9	■	●	■	■	■	■	■	■	■	7	8	10	12	■	
	Ricardo Rosset	(BRA)	Footwork-Hart FA17	9	■	■	11	■	■	■	■	11	■	11	8	9	■	14	13	
	Giancarlo Fisichella	(ITA)	Minardi-Ford M195B	■	-	-	13	■	■	■	8	■	11	-	-	-	-	-	-	
	Pedro Lamy	(POR)	Minardi-Ford M195B	■	10	■	12	9	■	■	■	12	■	12	■	10	■	16	12	
	Luca Badoer	(ITA)	Forti-Ford FG01B	NQ	11	■	NQ	10	■	NQ	■	NQ	-	-	-	-	-	-	-	
	Andrea Montermini	(ITA)	Forti-Ford FG01B	NQ	■	10	NQ	NQ	▲	NQ	■	■	NQ	-	-	-	-	-	-	
	Tarso Marques	(BRA)	Minardi-Ford M195B	-	■	■	-	-	-	-	-	-	-	-	-	-	-	-	-	
	Giovanni Lavaggi	(ITA)	Minardi-Ford M195B	-	-	-	-	-	-	-	-	-	-	NQ	■	NQ	■	15	NQ	

POINTS SCORING SYSTEM

FIRST	*ten points*	FOURTH	*three points*
SECOND	*six points*	FIFTH	*two points*
THIRD	*four points*	SIXTH	*one point*

SYMBOLS

■	driver retired from race	♦	pole position
●	driver disqualified	*	fastest race lap
▲	driver did not start race	NQ	did not qualify

1996 Constructors' Cup

1	Williams-Renault	175	4	McLaren-Mercedes	49	7	Sauber-Ford	11
2	Ferrari	70	5	Jordan-Peugeot	22	8	Tyrrell-Yamaha	5
3	Benetton-Renault	68	6	Ligier-Mugen	15	9	Footwork-Hart	1

BULL'S EYE! Damon Hill achieved his life's ambition by winning the Japanese GP to wrap up the 1996 World Championship

ANALYSIS OF THE 1997 SEASON

Williams for the cup

Almost invincible in 1996, Williams start as favourites, yet Ferrari, Benetton and McLaren are going to push them harder this year. Watch out too for the metamorphosis of Arrows.

Can anyone beat Williams? That is the question. Judging by their 1996 record of winning the Constructors' Cup thanks to their drivers Damon Hill and Jacques Villeneuve scoring 12 wins from the 16 Grands Prix, plus 12 pole positions and 11 fastest laps, it's unlikely that anyone will topple this mighty British team in the season ahead.

However, a winter is a long time in Formula One, and only when the cars hit the track for the first Grand Prix can one really judge the true potential of the latest crop of cars, the 1997 challengers. Only then can race fans judge how effective a job the designers, technicians and aerodynamicists have done on the new cars.

Close season testing will have given an indication about who is quick and who is not, but over the years there have been some stunning testing results that have led to nothing when it counted. But, on the other hand, certain teams have been known to run

their cars underweight in testing so they could set a fast time and encourage a potential sponsor to sign on the dotted line on a contract. Shameless business this motor racing, but never dull...

Such was the superiority of last year's Williams FW18, however, that designer Adrian Newey had an excellent base from which to design this year's car. And, don't forget that if the other designers manage to make the quantum leap in performance and make their new cars as good as the FW18, they'll still be lagging behind, as the new Williams FW19 is sure to be better still.

But then, late last year, dramatic news threatened the Williams team's potential dominance. Newey said he wanted to quit the team after a disagreement about its internal workings. He wanted out, and there was a large amount of cash being offered to join McLaren to help it back into the winner's circle in 1997. But Williams served an injunction to prevent Newey working elsewhere.

One of the endlessly interesting things about Formula One is that it never stands still. When regulations have been introduced in the past to slow the cars down, it's only been a matter of time before the designers have worked out ways to make their next cars as quick as before, even with these restrictions. Many of their innovative findings to achieve this goal then filter down to the automotive industry and on to road cars.

Not only was last year's Williams the best chassis, but in the Renault V10 it had one of the best engines, which exposed the weaknesses of the Benetton B196 chassis, as that too used the same Renault power plant yet was nowhere near the ultimate pace, despite having drivers of the calibre of Jean Alesi and Gerhard Berger at the wheel.

Many said the Benetton was hampered by being suitable for Michael Schumacher's idiosyncratic driving style, which is such that the car feels very nervous in corners, and that in the hands of anyone other than Schumacher, it was a particularly tricky beast. Expect this year's B197 to be more driver friendly.

However, if the Benetton was not a great car in 1996, neither where the Ferrari nor the McLaren. Sure, those drivers at the tail end of the grid would have been more than happy to be pedalling them, but next to the Williams, the ultimate benchmark, they were found wanting. Ferrari even made the comprehensive change from low nose format to high nose during the season, an alteration which is almost unheard of in Formula One circles. The once-mighty Prancing Horse was simply that desperate to catch up.

Anxious for success, the new Arrows is bound to go better than any of its predecessors, and look too for an improved showing from Jordan. Indeed, last year's car was not a classic and designer Gary Anderson started on the 1997 replacement as early as last summer, so expect it to be a major step forward for the team from Silverstone.

It's not all about having a good chassis in Formula One though, for the engine in the back has a vital part to play, too. Williams can be sure that its Renault is more than capable, with Benetton equally confident. But rumour has it that the Ferrari, Mercedes (in the McLarens) and the Peugeot (in the Jordans) may even push out more horsepower when pressed.

The Mugen in the Ligiers is also highly rated, while Ford is going to have to come up with something special to propel those new Stewarts up the road. And Yamaha will have to make engines that don't keeping blowing up to keep Damon Hill and new Arrows boss Tom Walkinshaw happy.

It's always a juggling act over the winter as all the variables are toyed with, but even more so than at the start of a new football season, the top teams are expected to come out with all guns blazing and carry on where they left off. The smaller teams may have found a new benefactor and have some new bits to show off, but it's been a long while since anyone other than Williams, Ferrari, Benetton and McLaren were in the top four.

MAYBE IN 1997: Members of the pit crew from Jacques Villeneuve's Williams team watch the monitor as their man sheds a wheel and drops out of the 1996 Japanese GP

Rothmans
Williams RENAULT
Australian Grand Prix, Albert Park

1	Race / Circuit	High
2	Wing level	High
3	Downforce	Rarely used and dusty, quite bumpy. Hard on brakes with mostly medium-speed turns. Low grip level with changes in asphalt on different sections
4	Circuit characteristics	
		Intermediate springs and roll-bars
5	Settings	

3.27miles/5.27km

The art of setting up an F1 car lies in finding the right blend of straightline speed, downforce, handling and grip – balancing left to right, front to rear and all points in-between. Tim Preston and Jock Clear, engineers to Damon Hill and Jacques Villeneuve in 1996, who between them won 12 of last year's 16 races, reveal all ...

TYRES: Normally set at 22psi front, 18psi rear, pressure is critical within a tolerance of 0.2psi. Pre-heating of tyres is controlled to maintain correct pressure when at full racing temperature (around 110°C). Too much pressure increases tyre degradation, resulting in a dramatic loss of performance. Pressures may be adjusted during qualifying or pitstops to improve handling.

ENGINE: Engine-management systems are set to produce specific performance characteristics for the circuit – Williams has 10 Renault engines at each meeting just in case!

GEARBOX: Ratios are tailored to suit individual circuit demands.
• *Engine and gearbox are both changed between qualifying and the race, and completely stripped and rebuilt after it.*

WINGLETS: These devices offered efficient downforce generation ahead of rear wheels and helped reduce wheel drag.
• *1997 technical regulations have ruled out the use of winglets by increasing the bodywork 'exclusion area' around the rear wheels*

REAR WINGS: Multiple setting 'holes' allow top three-blade wing assembly angle to be adjusted up (less wing) to reduce downforce, or down (more wing) to increase it. Several assemblies are available – each for a particular type of circuit and each configuration providing its own downforce parameters.

On high downforce circuits, the art of rear wing aerodynamics is in creating sufficient downforce without generating 'drag'. Additionally, a temporary aerodynamic strip, or counterflap, can be added for wet starts, giving the equivalent of one more 'hole' of wing.

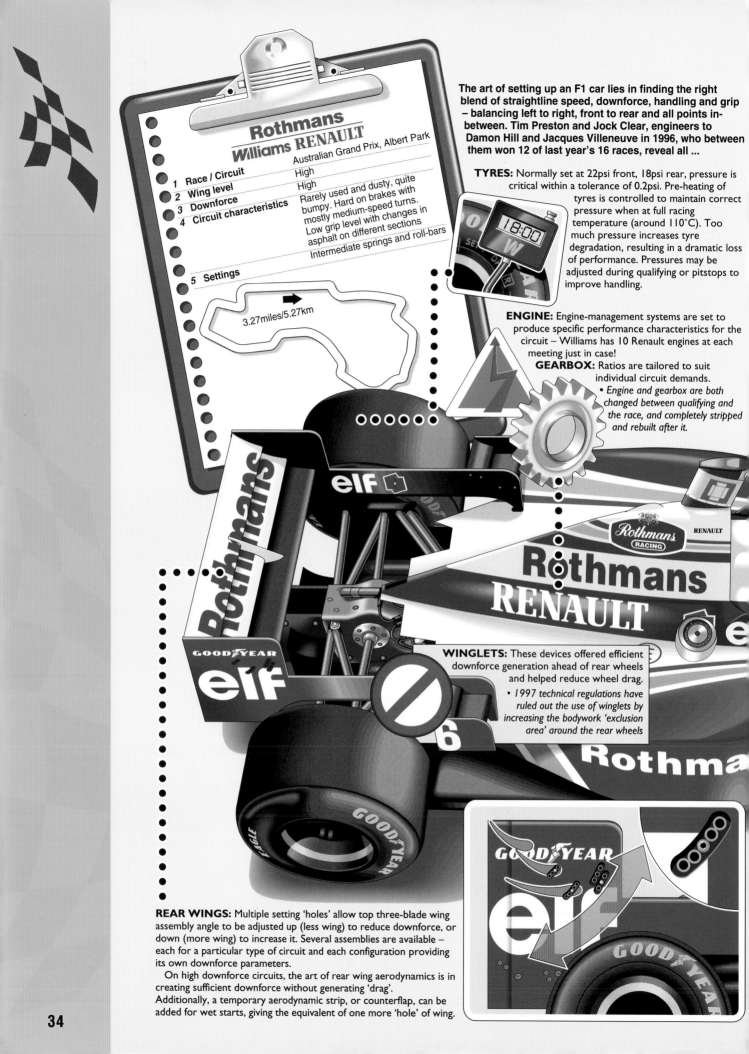

THE WINNING FORMULA

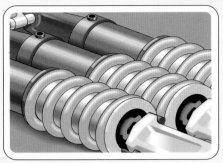

BRAKE WEAR
Race start:
28mm discs
Race finish:
20-21mm

▢ Wear

BRAKE DISCS:
Three thicknesses of carbon fibre discs are available – 24, 26 or 28mm. The faster the circuit, the more aggressive the braking, the thicker the disc used. Disc wear can amount to as much as 30% in a race.

BRAKE PADS:
One of the few 'single options' – 21mm. Wear on pads is much less severe at around 3mm.

SUSPENSION:
Take your pick!
The key is to select the right combinations of springs, dampers, wishbones, roll-bars, bump-rubbers... Key factors in determining the right 'mix' are in the specific circuit characteristics. Final adjustments are made once race strategy is decided. Total suspension travel, typically, is 25mm on the front, with around twice that on the rear.

• 'Aerodynamic' suspension arms, which appeared in the later stages of 1996, are restricted in 1997.

FRONT WINGS: Balance between front and rear is critical. Multiple setting and blade options again allow fine tuning.
• At anything above 100mph, enough downforce is generated to 'stick' the car upside down!

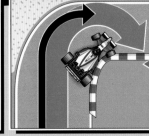

On the right track – Drivers are often heard complaining of *understeer* or *oversteer* – particularly when they have just dumped a few million pounds-worth of hardware in the kitty litter. But what causes these unwanted excursions, and what can be done to avoid them?

Understeer
An imbalance – lack of grip – at the front end causes car to turn in too slowly, forcing driver into wider line.
Causes: Too little front wing. Front suspension too stiff.
Correction: Increase front wing. Soften roll-bars, damping or spring levels. Lower front ride-height. Reduce front tyre pressure.

Oversteer
An imbalance to the rear results in turn-in becoming too sharp.
Causes: Too little rear wing. Rear suspension too stiff.
Correction: Increase rear wing. Soften rear suspension settings. Lower rear ride-height. Reduce rear tyre pressure.

IN THE PITS

Formula One folk knew nothing of refuelling until the rules were changed making it a part of every race, and further increasing the spectacle. And how it did at Hockenheim in 1994 when Jos Verstappen's Benetton was engulfed in flames from a tiny spillage. Pit-stops are safer now, but the crews still cross their fingers.

Pit stops for topping up fuel became part of Formula One as the racing had become processional, with little overtaking. Indeed, many Grands Prix saw the field run almost in grid order for the entire 200-mile distance. The purist could watch each race and appreciate the technical merits of each driver's performance. But a newcomer was unlikely to consider Formula One the most exciting sport ever witnessed and thus not likely to become one of the ranks of fans.

So, over the winter of 1993, the

−1 lap: Crew take up positions as driver passes pit and gets signal to come in at end of next lap

−30 seconds: Tyre blankets come off as late as possible to minimize loss of heat and pressure
Tyres are pre-heated to around 90°C

−16.3 seconds: Driver enters pit lane and activates limiter to keep within speed limit

120 kmh

S T O P !

0.2 seconds: Air-hammers are in place on wheel nuts
1.0 second: Front and rear jacks in position, car is raised

1.5 seconds: Fuel hose is connected. Red light shows in refueller's helmet to indicate fuel is flowing

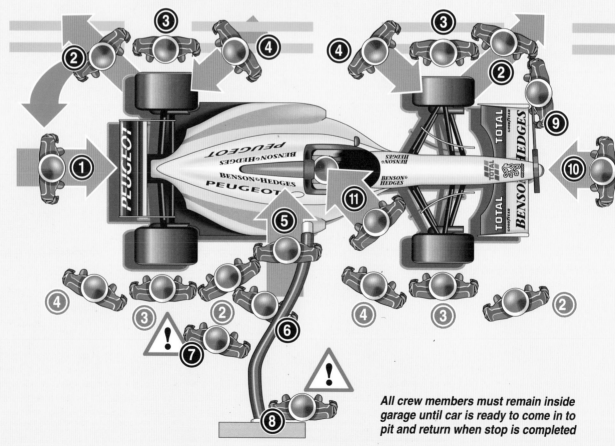

All crew members must remain inside garage until car is ready to come in to pit and return when stop is completed

powers-that-be decided to do something about it and make Formula One more exciting. So they passed a ruling that no Formula One car would have a fuel tank large enough to run a full Grand Prix without stopping. This, they reckoned, would shake up the order, and force the quickest drivers to have to overtake the slower cars several times as they made up ground again after their pit stops.

But, the trouble is, they also added danger to an already risky sport, as it is an immutable fact that hot engines and

a drop of fuel do not go together. Add one to the other and you will have a flash fire. Just ask Verstappen and his pit crew. After all, when they goofed in the 1994 German Grand Prix, they only leaked as little as 10 litres of fuel out of the nozzle and on to the side of the car. But it splashed on to the hot engine and in an instant they were engulfed by an inferno that shot 20 feet in the air. Rapid work by the crew with fire extinguishers had the flames out in six to seven seconds, during which time the Dutch driver popped his seatbelts

and escaped with minor burns to his face. Three of the crew were also injured. But it was a miraculous escape. The nozzles were then made safer for subsequent races.

So, when you watch these mid-race stops, remember that the crews have the pressure not only of refuelling the car as quickly as possible while their team-mates swap the tyres, but that they have the spectre of a flame-out always hanging over them. This is the real-time story of a Formula 1 pit stop with B&H Total Jordan Peugeot.

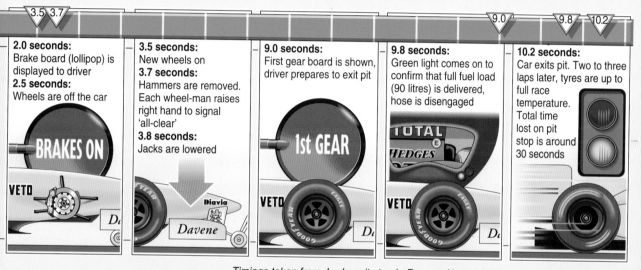

2.0 seconds:
Brake board (lollipop) is displayed to driver
2.5 seconds:
Wheels are off the car

3.5 seconds:
New wheels on
3.7 seconds:
Hammers are removed. Each wheel-man raises right hand to signal 'all-clear'
3.8 seconds:
Jacks are lowered

9.0 seconds:
First gear board is shown, driver prepares to exit pit

9.8 seconds:
Green light comes on to confirm that full fuel load (90 litres) is delivered, hose is disengaged

10.2 seconds:
Car exits pit. Two to three laps later, tyres are up to full race temperature. Total time lost on pit stop is around 30 seconds

Timings taken from Jordan pit stop in Buenos Aires, 1996, running a one-stop strategy

Pit crew 'who's who'...

1: **Rear jack** Follows car in, raises rear end
2: **Wheel off** Removes used wheels
3: **Hammer** Removes and fixes wheel nuts
4: **Wheel on** Positions new wheel
Man on left rear then goes to back of car and stands by with starter
5: **Refueller** Delivers pre-set fuel load

6: **Hose support** Steadies hose to allow safe refuelling
7: **Fireman** Stands by with fire extinguisher
8: **Rig minder** Operates 'dead-man's handle', which cuts fuel flow in emergency
9: **Brake board** Gives driver stop and go instructions
10: **Front jack** Raises front end of car
11: **Visor wipe** Cleans driver's helmet visor

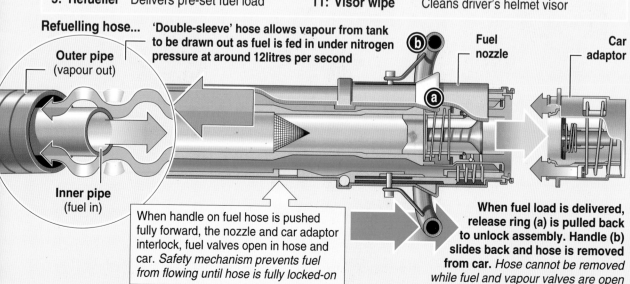

Refuelling hose... 'Double-sleeve' hose allows vapour from tank to be drawn out as fuel is fed in under nitrogen pressure at around 12 litres per second

Outer pipe (vapour out)

Inner pipe (fuel in)

Fuel nozzle

Car adaptor

When handle on fuel hose is pushed fully forward, the nozzle and car adaptor interlock, fuel valves open in hose and car. *Safety mechanism prevents fuel from flowing until hose is fully locked-on*

When fuel load is delivered, release ring (a) is pulled back to unlock assembly. Handle (b) slides back and hose is removed from car. *Hose cannot be removed while fuel and vapour valves are open*

WILLIAMS

Going for number nine

The team to beat through the mid-1990s, everyone will be gunning to beat Williams in 1997. But it's unlikely that they will be toppled from the very top of the pile.

Run down to the bookies now and bet your shirt on this one: a Williams driver will win the 1997 Formula One World Championship. Sure, there may be outside bets such as Michael Schumacher and his Ferrari, but those blue and white Rothmans-liveried cars from Grove in Oxfordshire are sure to be the favourites when the grid assembles under starter's orders in Melbourne's Albert Park, for the first Grand Prix of the season. It's up to you to choose whether to put your hard-earned cash on Jacques Villeneuve or Williams's new signing Heinz-Harald Frentzen. Flip a coin to make your choice.

If, or maybe, when, Williams wins the Constructors' Cup at the end of this season, the proud British constructor will overtake Ferrari as the team with the most world titles despite the fact that Frank Williams introduced his team to Formula One some 23 years after the Italian giant joined the circus at the beginning, way back in 1950. Doing so will emphasise yet again how British-based teams are the best in Formula One.

Indeed, the chief challenge to the supremacy of the Oxfordshire-based team in the season ahead will most likely come from McLaren (operating from Surrey), Benetton

THE DRIVERS

Heinz-Harald Frentzen

Make or break year as Frank Williams braved public outcry in Britain by signing him to replace Damon Hill, so he'd better be pitching for the world title in his fourth season of Formula One, or he'll have failed. Famed for his natural speed, and touted as being faster than compatriot Michael Schumacher in their early days, he ought to be able to take the battle to team-mate Jacques Villeneuve. Will have to prove he can sort a car in testing.

Jacques Villeneuve

Served his Formula One apprenticeship almost too successfully for Damon Hill fans last year, and the challenge of winning the World Championship now lies in front of this laid-back Canadian. Will find it different in the more-pressured role of number one driver, especially as he will be expected to beat Frentzen, a friend when they raced in Japan. Look out for his unusual and invariably successful overtaking manoeuvres... A real racer.

(Oxfordshire) and Ferrari (Maranello, Italy). With the chasing and ambitious pack behind them including Jordan (Northamptonshire), Arrows (Oxfordshire), Tyrrell (Surrey) and Stewart Grand Prix (Buckinghamshire).

The car to have

Enjoying the renowned world-beating skills of chief designer Adrian Newey, the new Williams FW19 is expected to be the class of the field as the FW18 was before it, handling competitively at every circuit, whether they possess fast and open corners or those tight and twisty slow bends. The sight of the two Williams drivers being able to do just about whatever they wanted must have galled their opponents as

HEROES OF THE PAST

Nigel Mansell

Revered by the man in the street for his bulldog attitude, but unpopular with insiders for his whinging. However, a charger through and through who gave his all to land a Lotus ride in 1980. Came close to winning in Monaco in 1984, but crashed. Joined Williams for 1985 and scored two wins. Pipped to world title in 1986 when tyre blew in Australia. Went to Ferrari for 1989 and 1990, but returned for final two years in Formula One with Williams, lifting title with nine wins in 1992 before heading to Indycars, in which he won 1993 crown.

FILL HER UP: Jacques Villeneuve sits patiently as the Williams crew does its business

they struggled to keep on the circuit in their vain fortnightly pursuit.

Add to this the Renault engine, and the package really starts to appeal. The French-built V10 was not the most powerful engine in the field last year, perhaps ceding that honour to Mercedes as the season progressed. But it was certainly right up there with the Ferrari and Peugeot. However, the Renault's power delivery was probably the pick of the pack, offering great driveability and, usefully, almost bullet-proof reliability. Thus, it's hardly surprising that the Williams-Renault is the dream package that all racing drivers would gnaw off their left hands to drive for a season.

Lest anyone has been out of town and not seen a newspaper for the last year or two, this will be Renault's final season in Formula One. Consequently, expect it to produce an engine that is good enough to ensure it leaves from the number one position.

However, Newey quit the team over the winter, angry at what he saw as his relative lack of power in the team's decision-making. This means the development of the car through the season will have to be done without the benefit of its creator. The basis of the design is so good though, that the Williams-Renault is almost certainly going to be the package to have again in 1997.

Keeping it together

One thing that Frank Williams will have to watch out for is the way he treats his drivers. For when he let it be known in the second half of last season that he would not be employing Damon Hill's services in 1997, just as Hill was shaping up to land the World Championship crown, the team and its personnel were greatly shaken. Indeed, Newey was so angered by the fashion in which his friend Hill had been treated that he let it be known that he was considering quitting the team and going to the rival McLaren camp. As proved the case in the close season.

Several years ago, this would have been a body blow to Williams, but it would not have been critical. However, Patrick Head, joint team principal with Frank Williams, has not been so involved with the cutting-edge design recently, so Newey's angry departure could yet prove to be a killer punch.

The team is most likely to be faced with one of its drivers landing the world title before the season is out, and it would be downright

TEAM VIPs

Frank Williams

Raced in Formula Three until he turned to team ownership in 1969, running a Formula One Brabham for Piers Courage. Struggled with lack of budget until landing Saudi backing in late 1970s and has since won eight Constructors' Cups. Confined to wheelchair since being crippled in a road accident in 1988.

Patrick Head

The son of a gentleman racing driver, Patrick started as a designer at Lola in 1970 and progressed via various projects to become Frank Williams's partner in Williams Grand Prix Engineering in 1976, designing FW07 chassis with which Alan Jones won the 1980 world title. Now more involved with operations than design.

KEEPING FIT: Jacques Villeneuve pounds the paddock in Australia

WHAT DOES THIS MEAN? Jacques Villeneuve takes a look at the telemetry in the pit garage at Hockenheim

FOR THE RECORD

Country of origin:	England
Team base:	Grove, England
Founded:	1969
Active in Formula One:	From 1973
Grands Prix contested:	364
Grand Prix wins:	96
Pole positions:	99
Fastest laps:	102
Constructors' Cup victories:	1980, 1981, 1986, 1987, 1992, 1993, 1994, 1996

Drivers and Results 1996

Driver	Nationality	Races	Wins	Pts	Pos
Damon Hill	English	16	8	97	1st
Jacques Villeneuve	Canadian	16	4	78	2nd

Car specifications 1997

Sponsors:	Rothmans
Team principal:	Frank Williams
Technical director:	Patrick Head
Team manager:	Dickie Stanford
Chief engineer:	Tim Preston
Drivers:	Heinz-Harald Frentzen & Jacques Villeneuve
Chassis:	Williams FW19
Engine:	Renault V10
Tyres:	Goodyear

dangerous to reject the future services of a world champion for the fourth time, following the dismissals of Nigel Mansell (champion in 1992), Alain Prost (1993) and Hill (1996).

After an element of friction was introduced between drivers Hill and Villeneuve last year as the championship unfolded, it will be intriguing to watch how this year's pairing of Villeneuve and Frentzen get on together.

However, they start the season with one advantage over other teams drivers; they are friends from living and racing in Japan at the same time in the early 1990s. Nonetheless, when the pressure is on, little chinks in the armour may appear, as the team divides itself into the competing camps that tend to form when you have two drivers of roughly equal ability as these two ought to be.

Frank Williams will have to watch out for internecine battling as each driver tries to assume superiority. However, if managed properly, this internal competition can help produce that extra little bit of speed that keeps the challenge of other teams at bay. After all, the one driver that any racer has to beat above all others is his team-mate...

Williams won an impressive 12 of the 16 Grands Prix in 1996. This year though it would not be unreasonable to only expect a tally of around nine in 1997, as more competitive packages from Benetton and McLaren join Ferrari in the chase.

THE BOSS: Frank Williams is the motivator, the man who built the team up from nothing

FERRARI

The Prancing Horse is hot to trot

Ferrari paid millions for Michael Schumacher in 1996, but the team didn't give him a hope of championship glory. This year, it's make or break for racing's most famous team.

The regular sight of a smoking Ferrari pulling to the side of the track last year may have caused personnel from the less well-funded teams to snigger, but it was not one that real fans of Formula One wanted to see. For everyone wants to see Ferrari at the sharp end in Formula One, as history has shown that when Ferrari is strong, so is the sport. To win without Ferrari would be like winning the football World Cup without Brazil participating. Ferrari is the class act and the great tradition, but not, of late, the icing on the cake.

Even though Michael Schumacher stressed that 1996 was a season simply for learning – perhaps winning a couple of Grands Prix – 1997 would be the push for the World Championship, last year was a huge disappointment. This year simply must be

NUMBER TWO: Eddie Irvine fitted in compliantly at Ferrari in 1996. With testing he should shine in 1997

FERRARI IN HARMONY: The pit crew work frantically to get Michael Schumacher back out on to the track in his epic race to victory in Spain

better. If Williams, Benetton and McLaren can not be caught, and beaten, then heads will roll within the ranks of the most famous team.

Tools of the trade

Funded by the gargantuan Fiat motor corporation, Italy's largest employer, there is always a budget for whatever the team needs. Add to this the fact that Marlboro and Shell take care of the drivers' wages, this leaves the team with ample money to develop its cars in whatever way they want. And it saved Ferrari £20m last year in Michael Schumacher's pay packet alone.

This year, Schumacher will again be the number one driver and Ulsterman Eddie Irvine will remain as the team's number two, giving precious continuity and certainly no lack of speed behind the wheel.

This arrangement will also mean the team has a pair of drivers with healthy mutual respect, one of the few pairings in Formula One

THE DRIVERS

Michael Schumacher

Acknowledged as the best in the business. Unbelievably fast, he always has the upper hand over his team-mates. One of the few drivers who can make a slow car fast, he did all Ferrari could have wanted and more in 1996. Possesses not only blinding speed in all conditions, but also the best tactical brain in Formula One and the ability to drive to his maximum for the full two hours. Builds the team around himself, and it shows.

Eddie Irvine

Surprised everyone on his debut at Suzuka in 1993 when he re-passed Senna and earned a punch on the nose for his temerity. Surprised everyone a second time by joining Schumacher at Ferrari in 1996. Has natural speed and is more serious than his cavalier attitude suggests. Suffered from being allowed only a fraction of the testing time that Schumacher got last year. Will never be more than number two at Ferrari, but he's enjoying life.

DRIVE OF THE YEAR: Vile conditions brought out Schumacher's best in Spain. And he won in a chassis that didn't deserve his talent

TEAM VIPs

Jean Todt

Latter-day Napoleon who has brought order, and much-needed success, to the politically-riven Ferrari camp. Started life as a rally co-driver before becoming head of Peugeot-Talbot Sport and leading it to numerous wins in sportscars, rallies and desert raids. Took over Ferrari's competition side in 1993.

John Barnard

Illustrious and notoriously fiery British designer who produced the classic carbon-fibre MP4 chassis that served McLaren so well in the mid-1980s. Has headed the design teams at Ferrari, Benetton and then Ferrari again, even convincing Ferrari that he should have his design office in England.

HEROES OF THE PAST

John Surtees

To win a World Championship is an outstanding feat. But to do so both on two wheels and on four is extraordinary. Step forward John Surtees. This gifted Englishman won seven motorcycle World titles before he was coaxed into cars. Coming in second in only his second Grand Prix, John was signed by Ferrari in 1963 and became a winner before the year was out. However, he did more than shine on the track, as he galvanised the team and won the 1964 World title. A clash of characters saw him leave in 1966. After a successful spell with Honda, he formed his own team.

that appear to get on and assist, rather than obstruct the progress of the other.

But what of the car they will drive, will it be good enough in their quest for Formula One's holy grail? Last year's John Barnard-designed F310 chassis was truly radical. However, it was too radical, for not only was the car not ready until just before the season's opening Grand Prix, thus allowing the drivers almost none of the crucial pre-season testing, but also it was found to be relatively uncompetitive once the

season got underway. And so, amid much wringing of hands (and maybe of necks), the chassis had to be changed mid-season with the adoption of the high-nose shape favoured by others. So the entire team played "catch-up" through the season.

To make matters worse in 1996, the drivers couldn't even make up for it with the usual dollop of Ferrari power. Running with a 10-cylinder engine for the first time in place of the V12s that had been Ferrari's backbone almost

FOR THE RECORD

Country of origin:	Italy
Team base:	Maranello, Italy
Founded:	1939
Active in Formula One:	From 1950
Grands Prix contested:	572
Grand Prix wins:	108
Pole positions:	118
Fastest laps:	124
Constructors' Cup victories:	1961, 1964, 1975, 1976, 1977, 1979, 1982, 1983

Drivers and Results 1996

Driver	Nationality	Races	Wins	Pts	Pos
Michael Schumacher	German	16	3	59	3rd
Eddie Irvine	Northern Irish	16	0	11	10th

Car specifications 1997

Sponsors:	Marlboro, Shell, Pioneer, Asprey
Team principal:	Jean Todt
Team manager:	Claudio Berro
Designers:	John Barnard & Ross Brawn
Chief engineer:	Giorgio Ascanelli
Drivers:	Michael Schumacher & Eddie Irvine
Chassis:	Ferrari F310B
Engine:	Ferrari V10
Tyres:	Goodyear

those beyond. Indeed, many at Ferrari will be delighted to have the team's brains in Italy, as Barnard's insistence on having his design studio located in England was never adjudged a success, precipitating dire internal power struggles. Don't forget that the Ferrari team has always been encumbered by a strong Machiavellian streak.

Pressures at home

The pressure to succeed is huge, and Ferrari is watched with greater scrutiny than people outside Italy can comprehend. In Italy, Ferrari is Formula One. Newspapers employ journalists specifically to fill their pages daily with news on Ferrari. Any news will do, and thus some is fanciful to put it mildly. When the team hits a rut, everyone knows about it. Indeed, team boss Jean Todt was under pressure to resign when the red cars kept retiring in 1996. At times last summer, the fervent *tifosi* were crying for his head. Admirably, Schumacher came to his defence, saying: "if you want to destroy Ferrari, then kick out Todt." He is right, for the little Frenchman is one of the best organisers in the business, and no team needs organising like Ferrari.

If Todt succeeds, then the team will be back where it belongs. If he doesn't, stories of Fiat pulling the plug on Ferrari's racing division will surface again, leaving the great marque with just its road cars to build. However, Fiat boss Gianni Agnelli has been converted into such a Schumacher fan that last November he made the German sign on the dotted line to stay as Ferrari's lead driver through until the end of the 1999 season, by which time he may well have landed another World Championship. One thing is certain; whatever the results on the track, his precocious talents will have made him the wealthiest sportsman in the world.

since racing began, it was clear that Ferrari's prancing horsepower was only as much, or even (whisper it) slightly less, than the regular horsepower of its competitors. Only Michael Schumacher's extraordinary prowess kept his Ferrari in the ballpark with Williams, Benetton and McLaren, with his victory in the Spanish Grand Prix down to his extraordinary skills in the wet rather than the car being the best in the field that day. The two wins that followed later in the year, which came in the Belgian and – joy of joys – the Italian Grands Prix, were pleasingly down to a clear improvement in the car.

This year's chassis is a derivation of the F310 in the form that it finished last season, hopefully with the gremlins sorted out. With the drivers already testing new development parts for it before last season came to an end, the odds are that the team will be starting at full speed this year. But remember, Ferrari has had many a false dawn.

What else has changed? Well, Barnard's contract runs only to this July, and former Benetton designer Ross Brawn is joining the team, and most expect him to be in charge of the 1998 Ferrari and

FERRARI'S FIELD MARSHAL: Jean Todt, the man who has led Ferrari back to the winner's circle

BENETTON

Life after Schumacher

EXPERIENCED ATTACK:
Gerhard Berger and Jean Alesi must prove that experience counts in 1997

This former superteam is desperate to claw its way back into the winner's circle that it used to visit so often with Michael Schumacher in 1995.

THE DRIVERS

Jean Alesi

Signed from Ferrari to replace Michael Schumacher when he crossed over for the 1996 season. It was thought this was the fiery Frenchman's big shot at the world title. Well, if it was, he blew it, and team boss Flavio Briatore was not always impressed with what he saw, to put it mildly, even talking of kicking Jean out. Jean is fast enough, but he may not think quickly enough to convert this into a championship.

Gerhard Berger

Also joined Benetton last year, teaming up again with Jean Alesi when he couldn't face the thought of partnering Michael Schumacher at Ferrari. Initially he couldn't fit the car, but came on strong in the second half of the year when, against the form book, he was the quicker Benetton driver. Tends to use his head a lot more than Alesi does, so will be far more of a title threat if this year's car comes good.

Benetton had better start winning Grands Prix again in the season ahead, and lots of them, or team owner Flavio Briatore will get angry. Very, very angry…

Indeed, the man who was famous for his ear-to-ear grin, backward-turned baseball cap and extravagant hugging of Michael Schumacher through 1994 and 1995, was not generally good company last season. The cap worn back to front remained, but the jaunty stride down the pitlane was gone and the white-toothed smile was definitely a thing of the past as Williams, and even Ferrari, did the winning. Worst of all, his Benetton team was knocked from first to third place in the Constructors' Cup.

Most Formula One teams would be delighted to have finished third in the Constructors' Cup, but not Benetton. Especially as it had been the top team in 1995 and it had been lying in second place until the final Grand Prix. But, its drivers Gerhard Berger and, in

MERCURIAL TALENT: Jean Alesi was fast but prone to mistakes in 1996, failing to win a Grand Prix for Benetton, which almost cost him his seat for 1997

HEROES OF THE PAST

Nelson Piquet

A treble World Champion, but not a driver who was regarded as an ambassador for the sport. Nelson didn't arrive at Benetton for his two-season stay until the end of his 203-race Grand Prix career. The Brazilian's glory days were with Brabham, for whom he drove from 1979 to 1985, picking up the 1981 and 1983 world titles. The next two years were spent at Williams, with Nelson champion again in 1987 before moving to Lotus for 1988 and 1989. His spell at Benetton produced two wins in 1990 and one in 1991, then he went to race in Indycars and had a huge shunt in the 1992 Indy 500.

TEAM VIPs

Flavio Briatore

Came into Formula One in 1989 after establishing Benetton's clothing business in the USA. Not only has he managed Benetton since then, including guiding Michael Schumacher to 1994 and 1995 world titles, but he also owns stakes in Ligier and Minardi teams. Briatore is flamboyant and loves to surround himself with glamorous women.

Nick Wirth

Elevated to Benetton's chief designer after departure of Ross Brawn at end of last year. Amazingly ran his own Formula One team, Simtek, when still in his 20s, but it went bankrupt and he moved across to Benetton's design team. At 6ft 6ins he is the tallest man in Formula One.

particular, Jean Alesi, underperformed and let Ferrari move ahead.

To say that Briatore was hopping mad at Suzuka last October was an understatement. Alesi, who crashed out exiting the first corner on the opening lap, couldn't wait to flee the circuit and escape his boss's fury. Indeed, on several occasions through the 1996 season, the Italian boss threatened to cast the French driver out of the team for not delivering the goods. But, armed with a two-year contract, Alesi hung on. Despite this, Alesi spent most of the close season unsure of whether he would be staying on with Benetton after all; there was talk of a massive pay cut and even a move to Jordan (the team not the country). It was a messy business indeed.

The crux of the problem though, was that there had been no wins for Benetton for the first time since the 1988 season, when Alessandro Nannini and Thierry Boutsen also couldn't crack the big one. Benetton was third overall that year, too. Mind you, there had been an even greater domination in 1988 than Williams winning 12 of the 16 Grands Prix held last year: back then McLaren's Ayrton Senna and Alain Prost won fully 15 of the 16 races,

and Nannini's second place at the British Grand Prix was the best the team could manage.

A trying year

There were many problems within the team last season, the main one being that Berger couldn't fit into the 1995 chassis for close-season testing and both he and Alesi found the 1996 car awkward to drive. It was a development of the previous car that had been designed to suit the out-going Schumacher's unusual all-on-the-nose driving style.

Furthermore, it was later revealed that Berger had spent the first half of the year trying to shake off the after-effects of pneumonia. However, despite an ill-fated move that led to his retirement in the first race, Alesi was able to finish high enough to get on to the rostrum in the next two Grands Prix. Indeed, four times through the 16-race programme the French driver finished second and four times he was third. But never first in a season in which Alesi had been seen as the likely principal challenger to Hill.

As his health returned, it was Berger who came closer to success, and victory in the German Grand Prix should have been his, but his engine blew just a few laps from home, leaving Damon Hill to collect the extra four points that were to prove valuable in the run-in to the final round.

Berger also looked capable of sticking with Hill in the final round, but his ill-fated dive at the Englishman early in the race, the one that had British viewers gulping, bent his nose wing and the ensuing extra pitstop dropped him from what would have been second to an eventual fourth, helping his old team Ferrari go ahead for good in the Constructors' Cup. Indeed, in the final two Grands Prix, Berger twice came into contact with Eddie

Irvine's Ferrari, which is more the sort of behaviour one would have expected from a novice than from Formula One's most seasoned campaigner. And, in conjunction with Alesi's frequent red mists, this left Briatore wondering whether he might have done better building for the future by employing and developing a pair of rookie drivers.

A RARE SMILE: The frequently beaming face of Benetton boss Flavio Briatore more often wore a scowl in 1996

THWARTED AMBITION: Gerhard Berger failed to win a race in 1996, but came desperately close in Germany

The year ahead

So, what hopes are there for the year ahead? Well, like Williams, Benetton has Renault engines again, which is a definite plus point. But Briatore knows that this is the final time as the French automotive giant is pulling out of Formula One at the end of the season, feeling that its frequent successes in Formula One are no longer heeded by the public at large. People tend to remember that a Williams or (in 1995 at least), a Benetton has won a race, not that it had a Renault V10 in the back. Finding a replacement will not be easy.

As far as chassis design is concerned, designer Ross Brawn has moved on to pastures new, as has Rory Byrne after years of service, leaving the way clear for Nick Wirth to be promoted into this prime position. Not only is Wirth the tallest man in Formula One, but he is one of the brightest and worked wonders when he entered his own Simtek team when still in his twenties. It only lasted for just over a season before the withdrawal of a sponsor sent it under early in 1995. Having gone into liquidation, Wirth moved to Benetton to gain vital experience of working in a properly-funded team with world-beating facilities. This will be the first Benetton to bear his hallmark.

With Alesi and Berger's performances under intense scrutiny, they are sure to remember that Briatore has an increasing number of highly-rated young Italian drivers on his books ready to jump into any vacancy.

FOR THE RECORD

Country of origin:	England
Team base:	Enstone, England
Founded:	1986
Active in Formula One:	From 1986
Grands Prix contested:	236
Grand Prix wins:	26
Pole positions:	13
Fastest laps:	32
Constructors' Cup victories:	1995

Drivers and Results 1996

Driver	Nationality	Races	Wins	Pts	Posi
Jean Alesi	French	16	0	47	4th
Gerhard Berger	Austrian	16	0	21	6th

Car specifications 1997

Sponsors:	Benetton Sportsystem
Team principal:	Flavio Briatore
Team manager:	Joan Villadelprat
Designer:	Nick Wirth
Chief engineer:	Pat Symonds
Drivers:	Jean Alesi & Gerhard Berger
Test driver:	Alexander Wurz
Chassis:	Benetton B197
Engine:	Renault V10
Tyres:	Goodyear

McLAREN

Poised for victory

McLaren has not won a Grand Prix since 1993, and this hurts. But engine supplier Mercedes look set to be rewarded.

After a fruitless run lasting longer than he would care to discuss, McLaren boss Ron Dennis is giving his absolute all to win this year's Constructors' Cup. Nothing more, nothing less. If there's a driver's title thrown in for good measure for Mika Hakkinen or David Coulthard, then all the better. But the most important thing is to put McLaren back on the winning trail. It may well prove that the team will have to "do a Ferrari" and win two or three Grands Prix this year before making a full-blooded assault in 1998, but if you don't aim high, you'll never reach your goal.

Dennis's finest moment was back at the final race of 1993 when Ayrton Senna won the Australian Grand Prix to make McLaren the most successful Formula One team of all time, overtaking Ferrari to move to the head of the table of teams with the most Grand Prix victories; 104 to the Italian team's 103. The world is a cruel place, and Dennis and McLaren have not tasted the fruits of victory since, and

WAIT HERE! Mika Hakkinen in the pits

THE DRIVERS

Mika Hakkinen

Astounding people with the speed of his recovery from the head injury he suffered in the final Grand Prix of 1995, Mika knuckled down to developing the McLaren-Mercedes to the point at which it was in with a shout of winning races. And how Mika needs to win one, as his winless streak is one of the longest in Formula One history: this from a driver who was quicker than Michael Schumacher in Formula Three.

David Coulthard

David found it a shock going from race-winning Williams to the less-than-perfect McLaren at start of year. But he soon used his experience to claw his way on to Mika Hakkinen's pace, even out-racing the Finn in the second half of the year. This year they start equal, and the battle for supremacy will be most interesting. Needs to win races again to cement his reputation as one of the best of the current crop.

TEAM VIP

Ron Dennis

Ron started as a mechanic with Cooper, but don't remind him of this. He rose to top with Rondel then Project Four Formula Two teams, then bought McLaren in 1980. Took Formula One to new heights of professionalism, winning seven Constructors' Cups by 1991. Also builds the world-beating F1 GTR sportscar.

now lag behind Ferrari on victories again, and Williams are fast closing in on both teams.

A new sponsor

Even worse, McLaren has lost its long-standing sponsor Marlboro which is all but unthinkable. Think McLaren and you automatically think red and white livery in Marlboro's chevron shape. After all, the cars have been like that since Emerson Fittipaldi moved there from Lotus in 1974 and promptly landed his second World Championship title.

Frustrated by McLaren's three-season victory drought, Marlboro's parent company Philip Morris called it a day. And in its place for 1997 comes a new sponsor, West, also a tobacco brand that was previously seen in Formula One, albeit with the less than successful Zakspeed team in the late 1980s. West will find its second bash at Formula One far more professional in every way, and more successful too.

Although the financial hole has been filled, the divorce was extremely painful, showing everybody that this famous team is not as indestructible as it once was. Despite the fact that McLaren remains among the big four teams – along with Williams, Ferrari and Benetton – it is a very long way from 1988, when its drivers Ayrton Senna and Alain Prost amazingly won all but one of the year's 16 Grands Prix.

The vital ingredients

Taking the drivers first, both Hakkinen and Coulthard are a known quantity to the team, with the Finnish driver starting his fourth full campaign and the Scot his second. And they're rated as two of the top drivers in Formula One. That's one ingredient that should cause few hiccoughs in the season ahead. Providing, that is, they've learned from the error of their ways in last year's Portuguese Grand Prix at Estoril, where Hakkinen managed to spear his own team-mate off the circuit at one point. Indeed, both drivers were frustrated that day as their cars were off the pace. Give him a car capable of winning though, as he was in last year's Belgian and Italian Grands Prix, and he is able to focus fully and race with the best out there.

Coulthard, on the other hand, is a bit more sure of himself and more dependable under pressure, and not once last year did he make the mistake of spinning off on the parade lap at the start of the race, as he did in 1995. That's a bit like tripping up when running on to the pitch for a football cup final.

Like its predecessor, the new MP4/12 chassis comes from the pen of Neil Oatley, leader of McLaren's design team. And, providing he has sorted the problems last year's MP4/11 had negotiating mid-speed and low-speed corners, then the team will be able to start closing the gap to

the dominant Williams-Renaults. After all, far too many of the modern-day Grand Prix circuits are made up of more mid-speed and low-speed corners than the glorious high-speed sweepers of bygone years. Oatley's task is certain to be helped by the arrival of defecting ace Williams designer Adrian Newey.

McLaren's power comes from a Mercedes V10 and this engine proved itself to have as much grunt as any one of the other top engines last season. Perhaps even more as the season unfolded, as it excelled on high-speed circuits such as Hockenheim and Monza, with Coulthard being clocked at just under a mind-boggling 222mph down one of the straights in qualifying for the German Grand Prix.

While Mercedes has thus far been prepared to play the role of the benevolent parent wanting its child to develop in its own good time, one gets the impression that crawling is out, tottering is no longer on the agenda and only a full-blooded sprint will do. Especially as its prestigious International Touring Car Championship shop window was closed last autumn and its success in Indycars was a shadow of its former self in 1996 as Honda came in and took control. Success in Formula One is essential to Mercedes in 1997. And everyone at McLaren, from Dennis down, knows this means winning Grands Prix. Preferably lots of them.

FOR THE RECORD

Country of origin:	England
Team base:	Woking, England
Founded:	1963
Active in Formula One:	From 1964
Grands Prix contested:	445
Grand Prix wins:	105
Pole positions:	79
Fastest laps:	69
Constructors' Cup victories:	1974, 1984, 1985, 1988, 1989, 1990, 1991

Drivers and Results 1996

Driver	Nationality	Races	Wins	Pts	Pos
Mika Hakkinen	Finnish	16	None	31	5th
David Coulthard	Scottish	16	None	18	7th

Car specifications 1997

Sponsors:	West, Mercedes, Mobil, Boss, TAG-Heuer
Team principal:	Ron Dennis
Team manager:	David Ryan
Designers:	Neil Oatley, Adrian Newey & Steve Nichols
Chief engineers:	David Brown & Steve Hallam
Drivers:	David Coulthard & Mika Hakkinen
Chassis:	McLaren MP4/12
Engine:	Mercedes V10
Tyres:	Goodyear

JORDAN

Many rivers to cross

Eddie Jordan thought he'd got Damon Hill to lead his team, but he lost him to the Arrows outfit and the Jordan team is left with a whole new line-up.

Results weren't falling into place for Jordan last season and they should have been, as the team was in its sixth year in Formula One and yet still fifth overall in the team rankings, as it had been in its first season in 1991. Still in with the second division of teams, still lodged behind the big four of Williams, Ferrari, Benetton and McLaren.

The Peugeot engines were known to be powerful, and drivers Rubens Barrichello and Martin Brundle were no slouches. Yet all too often they failed to finish Grands Prix as high up the order as was expected. So the chassis must have been to blame, and indeed designer Gary Anderson took time off midseason to make a start on the 1997 replacement so that a full winter of testing could be carried out.

Signing a Schumacher

The first part of the resurrection came when Ralf Schumacher was signed up as a publicity-guaranteeing number two driver towards the end of the 1996 season. Jordan didn't want either Barrichello or Brundle to stay, so the German would fit in well alongside Damon Hill. Wrong, Hill went to Arrows and Jordan had to get his skates on to find a replacement in a market denuded of top drivers. There was even the tease of 1992 World Champion Nigel Mansell signing. So, how the team will fare with the inexperienced duo of Schumacher and Giancarlo Fisichella will be interesting. After all, if no results come in 1997 for the want of a good number one, the team could lose its works engines, and the spiral tends to go down from there... But, never count the Silverstone-based team out.

IN THE GENES? This is Ralf Schumacher's chance to silence the doubters

FOR THE RECORD

Active in Formula One:	From 1991
Grands Prix contested:	99
Grand Prix wins:	None
Pole positions:	1
Fastest laps:	1

Drivers and Results 1996

Driver	Nationality	Races	Wins	Pts	Pos
Rubens Barrichello	Brazilian	16	None	14	8th
Martin Brundle	English	16	None	8	11th

Car specifications 1997

Sponsors:	Benson & Hedges
Team principal:	Eddie Jordan
Team manager:	John Walton
Designer:	Gary Anderson
Drivers:	Ralf Schumacher & Giancarlo Fisichella
Chassis:	Jordan 197
Engine:	Peugeot V10
Tyres:	Goodyear

THE DRIVERS

Ralf Schumacher

This year the world at large will find out if all the Schumacher talent went to Michael. Being a famous brother could be as difficult as being a famous son, like Damon Hill. However, winning last year's Formula Nippon title proves that there must be some ability there.

Giancarlo Fisichella

A karting ace, he caught the eye in Formula Three with Alfa Romeo, and is the young Italian star of the moment. The *tifosi* would love to see him become World Champion in a Ferrari. Their wait has been a long one: Italy's last World Champion was Alberto Ascari in 1953.

PROST

Waving the tricolour

France is desperate for its team to break into the big time and challenge those teams from the other side of the English Channel.

Ligier was a French team and proud of it. With Olivier Panis's stunning win against the run of play in last year's Monaco Grand Prix, it was also a winning team again, for the first time since Jacques Laffite won in Canada all the way back in 1981. However, the team's engines come from the Mugen company in Japan, and with Shinji Nakano so does its number two driver, again postponing the day when the team's dream of becoming all-French is realized.

Considering the Ligier team has been in Formula One since 1976, it has had an extraordinary number of changes of ownership in recent years. Owned since inception by former French rugby international Guy Ligier, it passed on to Cyril de Rouvre in 1992, after a move by former World Champion Alain Prost to take control failed.

The ownership game

Then things began to get interesting. De Rouvre was jailed for fraud and Benetton boss Flavio Briatore took over in 1994. Tom Walkinshaw grabbed the reins in 1996 and threatened to make the team move to Britain in a quest to make it more competitive. This rocked the French, as it would have left them without a Formula One team. However, Walkinshaw sold out and went to Arrows, leaving the way clear for Prost to make another bid with the backing of the French Minister of Sport and Peugeot. This time, however, it was successful and the team is now running under the name of Prost, with one-time Ferrari team boss Cesare Fiorio acting as team manager.

THE DRIVERS

Shinji Nakano

An accomplished driver, Shinji cut his teeth in karts, then Japanese Formula Three, before racing in Britain in 1990 and 1991, before going home to race in Formula Three and Formula 3000, finishing sixth overall for Dome last year.

Olivier Panis

Mr Dependable. Olivier is neither spectacular in or out of the car, he simply gets on with the job and doesn't make mistakes. But that's running in the midfield for you... On his day though, such as at Monaco last year, when the rain made everything equal, he showed that he deserves a better car.

FOR THE RECORD

Country of origin:	France
Team base:	Magny-Cours, France
Founded:	1971
Active in Formula One:	From 1976
Grands Prix contested:	328
Grand Prix wins:	9
Pole positions:	9
Fastest laps:	11

Drivers and Results 1996

Driver	Nationality	Races	Wins	Pts	Pos
Olivier Panis	French	16	1	13	9th
Pedro Diniz	Brazilian	16	None	2	15th

Car specifications 1997

Sponsors:	Gauloises
Team principal:	Alain Prost
Team manager:	Cesare Fiorio
Designer:	Loic Bigois & George Ryton
Chief engineer:	Andre de Cortanze
Drivers:	Shinji Nakano & Olivier Panis
Chassis:	Ligier JS45
Engine:	Mugen V10
Tyres:	Bridgestone

THE GLORY BOY: Winner Panis in 1996

53

SAUBER

Life without Frentzen

Frentzen is gone, but Malaysian money is in place to push Sauber back on course, this year armed with Ferrari engines.

Ferrari engines could make all the difference for the Sauber team this season. The coup of landing the ex-works Italian V10s was pulled off late last year, thanks to the financial clout of team sponsor Petronas, the Malaysian state oil company.

There have been other changes at the Swiss team, though. In seasons past, the one constant, apart from team owner Peter Sauber, was Heinz-Harald Frentzen. But now, after three seasons, he has gone to Williams, leaving the team to continue its quest for its first Grand Prix success. Will Sauber get any closer this year than its best ever placing of third, at Monza in 1995? Then it still had the luxury of half decent engines, using the Ford Zetec-R engine that Michael Schumacher had behind him when he won the world title for Benetton in 1994. It's all a question of how well the Sauber chassis can be made to work with the Italian horsepower.

Oriental influence

Designer Leo Ress is hoping that engine wizard and ex-Ferrari employee Osamu Goto will be able to make the package more competitive than last year's Ford-powered cars and give team leader Johnny Herbert and new team-mate Nicola Larini a chance to at least have a crack at challenging the big four teams. It should be noted that the Malaysian government is not going to do anything by half measures, as it's very keen to host a Grand Prix in the near future.

THE DRIVERS

Johnny Herbert

A team leader at last. This is a just and long overdue reward for a driver who has not received his dues in a chequered Formula One career. Now it's Johnny's turn to show the world that he can get serious and produce the goods with a team built around him. With the continuity of a two-year contract, he should blossom. But the lack of a top line engine could temper his speed

Nicola Larini

Many will be delighted with the return of this Italian from touring cars. Nicola first raced in Formula One in 1987, and even subbed for Ferrari in 1992 and 1994. The former Italian Formula Three champion will be quick if the package is right.

FOR THE RECORD

Country of origin:	Switzerland
Team base:	Hinwil, Switzerland
Founded:	1970
Active in Formula One:	From 1993
Grands Prix contested:	66
Pole positions:	None
Fastest laps:	None
Grand Prix wins:	None

Drivers and Results 1996

Driver	Nationality	Races	Wins	Pts	Pos
Heinz-Harald Frentzen	German	16	None	7	12th
Johnny Herbert	English	16	None	4	14th

Car specifications 1997

Sponsors:	Petronas & Red Bull
Team principal:	Peter Sauber
Team manager:	Beat Zehnder
Designer:	Leo Ress
Chief engineer:	Ernst Keller
Drivers:	Johnny Herbert & Nicola Larini
Chassis:	Sauber C16
Engine:	Ferrari V10
Tyres:	Goodyear

HERR SAUBER: Peter Sauber is one of Formula One's straight dealers

LOLA

Lola is back on the brink, again...

Lola is one of the world's leading racing car builders, yet its forays into Formula One have never hit the headlines. This one did not have the energy for lift-off.

FOR THE RECORD

Country of origin:	England
Team base:	Huntingdon, England
Founded:	1957
Active in Formula One:	From 1962–1963, 1974–1975, 1987–1991, 1993, 1997
Grands Prix contested:	125
Grand Prix wins:	None
Pole positions:	1
Fastest laps:	None
Constructors' Cup victories:	None

Car specifications 1997

Sponsors:	MasterCard
Team principal:	Eric Broadley
Team manager:	Ray Boulter
Designer:	Eric Broadley & Lola Design Team
Drivers:	Ricardo Rosset & Vincenzo Sospiri
Chassis:	Lola T97/30
Engine:	Ford V8
Tyres:	Bridgestone

British chassis specialist Lola is finally returning to Formula One after several years of discussion. How it will fare, nobody knows, but the deal only came together last November. So, armed with a chassis by Lola's in-house design team and powered by a Ford EC V8 engine, drivers Ricardo Rosset and Vincenzo Sospiri will have a steep learning curve.

Try, try and try again

Most people forget that Lola has been in Formula One before. Yet it has, several times and those with longer memories will recall when Eric Broadley built cars in 1962 for Team Bowmaker to enter for John Surtees and Roy Salvadori, with Surtees and Lola placing fourth overall. Lola was asked to build cars for Graham Hill's team in 1974 and continued into 1975 until Hill's own cars were ready. Then in 1985 and 1986, the grids were graced by Beatrice-Lolas, but these had no Lola involvement, save for the fact that Lola's American importer Carl Haas was behind the team.

In 1987, Lola was back, this time building cars for Larrousse, and the project soldiered through five seasons, peaking with sixth in the Constructors' Cup in 1990. The final "part-Lola" project was in 1993 when chassis were built for the Scuderia Italia team and, despite Ferrari engines, often failed to qualify. And few at Lola want to remember that troubled campaign.

Sadly, Lola's grand plans came to naught. They failed to qualify in Australia and the money ran out before Brazil, forcing the team to quit the championship, and putting the company in jeopardy.

SIGN ON THE LINE: Eric Broadley – "Mr Lola" – signs with MasterCard's Mava Heffler

THE DRIVERS

Ricardo Rosset

This former tri-athlete needs a project to get his teeth into after a disappointing debut season with Arrows. Should grow in stature if Lola progresses. Has a good, technical brain and ample natural speed, although both can be hidden when a driver is in one of the third division teams. He simply needs to regain lost confidence. Rumoured to have access to even more family wealth than compatriot Pedro Diniz.

Vincenzo Sospiri

Very laid-back and a pure racer, Vincenzo was stuck in Formula 3000 for years: He was Damon Hill's team mate in 1990, and took until 1995 to win the title. Always troubled raising a budget – the MasterCard deal ressurected the 1996 Benetton test driver's career.

TYRRELL

Hanging on in there

Once the top team in Formula One, now just an also-ran, Tyrrell will be fighting its usual battles and, as ever, chasing a big sponsor. It seems a long time since the glory days of the 1970s.

THE DRIVERS

Mika Salo

Already courted by several of the top teams for 1998, this spiky Finn will be looking to wring the most out of the Tyrrell chassis to make sure that he continues to impress the right people and thus won't be driving one again next year... Given a car with an engine that doesn't keep failing, as the Yamaha did in 1996, Mika ought to pick up more points, but sadly only for the minor placings.

Jos Verstappen

No-one has ever managed the progression from Karts to Formula One in as few races as this flying Dutchman. Snapped up by Benetton in 1994, Jos was pitched in at the deep end after the Finn Lehto broke his neck during pre-season testing. Although Jos didn't disgrace himself at Benetton – he claimed a highly impressive third place in the hungarian Grand Prix – he was dropped from the team. He has since raced for Simtek and Arrows.

Formula One motor racing is a transient and occasionally cyclical sport, but the Tyrrell team is like a backbone: it's a constant that helps to keep the whole Formula One package together. It's not glamorous, but it's dependable and – for close on three decades – it's always there.

Indeed, team owner Ken Tyrrell has been running his own team in Formula One for years longer than many of the current drivers have been alive. History relates that he started off as long ago as 1968 when this former Formula Three racer fielded the promising Jackie Stewart in a Matra.

Two seasons later, with one world drivers' championship title in the bag, Tyrrell's own chassis came on stream and in 1971 this famous pair claimed both the drivers' and the constructors' titles, with Stewart also winning the 1973 drivers' title before retiring from the sport. And with Stewart went Tyrrell's glory

BACK FOR MORE: Mika Salo is Tyrrell's trump card. But he needs results

TEAM VIP

Ken Tyrrell

Another former racer who turned to team management. Ken's team progressed to Formula One in 1968, winning drivers' title in 1969 with Jackie Stewart in a Matra. Started building his own chassis and won the 1971 Constructors' Cup. Has struggled on since 1983 without a win, and money is a perennial problem.

FORMULA ONE STALWART: Ken Tyrrell has seen it all and done it all. But his cars have not won a Grand Prix since 1983

days. Their time together produced 25 wins (with 15 in Tyrrell chassis as opposed to the Matras and Marches Stewart drove from 1968 through to 1970), while the subsequent 23 years have offered up just seven more, with the last of these coming in Detroit with Michele Alboreto at the wheel as long ago as 1983.

So, why does Tyrrell keeps pressing on? Each season proves harder than the last in the pursuit of glory, as ever larger budgets have to be found just to keep going, let alone to start progressing up towards the sharp end of the grid. The answer is simple: Ken Tyrrell is a racer, through and through, and can think of no other life. Except perhaps of spending more time watching Tottenham Hotspur play football.

Help from Japan

Mika Salo is staying on for a third season with Tyrrell and Ken hangs much of the team's hopes on this talented Finn, convinced that if designer Harvey Postlethwaite and technical director Mike Gascoyne can provide him with a good chassis, and Ford's new ED4 V8 engine proves both reliable and sufficiently powerful, that he will produce the goods and be a regular points scorer. The depressing fact is that if this happens, Salo is sure to move on to a more illustrious team for 1998.

Former Formula One *wunderkind* Jos Verstappen has moved across from Arrows to take over from Ukyo Katayama – a Tyrrell driver since 1993 – as Salo's number two. And part of the plan for the year ahead is that Japanese driver Toranosuke Takagi, a rising star in Formula Nippon (Japan's version of Formula 3000), will be the team's test driver, perhaps being offered a handful of race appearances at the end of this season as a precursor to a full season in 1998. He is a protégé of former Tyrrell driver Satoru Nakajima who is becoming more involved with the team and brings welcome backing from the Japanese PIAA automotive products group. All in all, this could be the start of a new era for the British team, as a regulated and consistent injection of investment is likely to make all the difference and will help propel the team to the front of the midfield pack.

FOR THE RECORD

Country of origin:	England
Team base:	Woking, England
Formed:	1960
Active in Formula One:	From 1970
Grands Prix contested:	387
Grand Prix wins:	23
Pole positions:	14
Fastest laps:	20
Constructors' Cup victories:	1971

Drivers and Results 1996

Driver	Nationality	Races	Wins	Pts	Pos
Mika Salo	Finnish	16	None	5	13th
Ukyo Katayama	Japanese	16	None	None	N/A

Car specifications 1997

Sponsor:	PIAA
Team principal:	Ken Tyrrell
Team manager:	Steve Nielsen
Designer:	Harvey Postlethwaite
Chief engineer:	Mike Gascoyne
Drivers:	Mika Salo & Jos Verstappen
Test driver:	Toranosuke Takagi
Chassis:	Tyrrell 025
Engine:	Ford ED4 V8
Tyres:	Goodyear

ARROWS

Tom's new hot shots

Tom Walkinshaw and shock signing Damon Hill will fire Arrows and Yamaha to new heights in their first season together.

When you think of Arrows this season, wipe all preconceptions from your mind, for Tom Walkinshaw's new team is as good as starting with a clean slate. It may have taken over the Arrows name, but it has nothing to do with the marque's unfortunate record of having contested the most races (some under the Footwork name) without winning a Grand Prix. For those into statistics, that's 288 races without a win or even a pole position or fastest lap. But that's the last time it needs mentioning.

On a far more constructive tack, Arrows – or new Arrows – has two main ingredients: World Champion Damon Hill and Walkinshaw. The former needs no introduction, but his tally of 21 wins from 67 Grand Prix starts is phenomenal. Add to this the fact that he's

TESTING, TESTING: Damon Hill puts Bridgetone's tyres through their paces

THE DRIVERS

Damon Hill

The Formula One World Championship is finally in the bag and Damon was able to relax over the winter, his lifelong target achieved. But now he has a new target, helping Tom Walkinshaw drag the revitalised Arrows team and Yamaha towards the front of the grid. Armed with the promising Bridgestone tyres and his renowned car developing skills, Damon could be precisely the man for the job. But don't expect race wins in 1997.

Pedro Diniz

He's rich and he's in Formula One, but he's better than people give him credit for. After his debut with Forti, he was thought of as a laughing stock. But the car was dreadfully slow and Pedro showed in 1996 at Ligier, that he's no fool. Clearly number two to Hill, but his budget has enabled him to learn in an improved environment.

MR BIG: Tom Walkinshaw is the driving force behind the Arrows revival. And he expects results

TEAM VIP

Tom Walkinshaw

Tough ex-racer who takes no prisoners and gets what he wants. Formed Tom Walkinshaw Racing in 1976 and has since run works touring car teams for Mazda, Jaguar, Holden and Volvo. Brought Jaguar great success in sportscars in the 1980s before moving into Formula One with Benetton. Masterminded Michael Schumacher's 1994 title, then took over Ligier before buying Arrows.

probably the best test and development driver currently in Formula One, and you can see what a coup Walkinshaw pulled off with his shock signing of Hill, when it was thought that he would end up at Jordan or even the new Stewart Grand Prix team after his sacking by Williams.

Walkinshaw may be less well known to you. But to say that he is a motorsport mogul would be an understatement. A former racer, he moved into management 21 years ago, mainly in saloon racing. But his list of clients grew rapidly as he was employed by BMW, Mazda, Jaguar – who he took to victory at Le Mans in 1988 – and Holden, before moving on to Formula One. He made his impact at Benetton, being the brains behind Michael Schumacher's world title in 1994. Hopefully Hill has forgiven him for that. Then he controlled Ligier, before he took over Arrows. The man has pedigree.

Making success happen

Not only has he coaxed Hill into signing up, but Yamaha too, snatching their engine deal from Tyrrell. And Walkinshaw has a way of convincing suppliers, partners as they are called, to raise their performance. So, expect to see these engines from Japan last full race distances in 1997 rather than going pop before the chequered flag has been waved, as they tended to do last year.

Frank Dernie is at the design helm. He has a long Formula One career behind him, having started with the Hesketh team back in 1976 before joining Williams, Lotus, Ligier and finally Benetton, where he also worked under Walkinshaw.

Walkinshaw has brought Pedro Diniz over from Ligier to act as a sound, and paying, number two driver. It will be a move that is good for both parties.

So, what chance success? Well, Walkinshaw is known to want to establish Arrows in the top six in 1997. That may not require race wins, but certainly rostrum finishes will be essential. And there have been precious few of those in the 21-year history of the Arrows team. Race wins are scheduled to follow in 1998 and a full-scale attack on the World Championship title in 1999. It may sound fanciful, but several gamblers will be more than happy to accept the wager. The season ahead will be an interesting one indeed, as the established top four teams joust for outright honours, and the three newcomers – Arrows, Lola, and Stewart Grand Prix – try and place themselves in the chasing group. Arrows, you feel, stand a good chance.

FOR THE RECORD

Country of origin:	England
Team base:	Witney, England
Founded:	1977
Active in Formula One:	From 1978
Grands Prix contested:	290
Grand Prix wins:	None
Pole positions:	None
Fastest laps:	None

Drivers and Results 1996

Driver	Nationality	Races	Wins	Pts	Pos
Jos Verstappen	Dutch	16	None	1	16th
Ricardo Rosset	Brazilian	16	None	None	N/A

Car specifications 1997

Sponsors:	Danka, Power Horse & Petrobras
Team principals:	Tom Walkinshaw
Team manager:	John Walton
Designer:	Frank Dernie
Drivers:	Pedro Diniz & Damon Hill
Test driver:	Jorg Muller
Chassis:	Arrows A18
Engine:	Yamaha V10
Tyres:	Bridgestone

MINARDI

Italy's other team

Ferrari has the money, Minardi has the enthusiasm. Year in, year out, this tiny Italian team of racers hangs in there, providing welcome variety but little more.

Minardi is perhaps the most admired team in Formula One. And not simply for keeping going in the face of continued financial adversity, but also for sticking to its policy of fielding talented drivers whenever possible. Sure there have been occasions when rent-a-drivers such as Giovanni Lavaggi have filled the cockpit, but only for as long as it takes until team owner Giancarlo Minardi says "basta" and puts one of his protégés back at the wheel. Elio de Angelis, Michele Alboreto, Alessandro Nannini and Giancarlo Fisichella all have cause to thank him for that. Put simply, Minardi is about racers going racing.

THE DRIVERS

Ukyo Katayama
Ukyo came to Formula One as Japanese Formula 3000 champion and as successor to Satoru Nakajima and moved on quickly from Larousse to Tyrrell in 1993. He stayed there for four seasons, impressing particularly in 1994, although never delivering the results. Booted out at the end of 1996, this is his last chance for Formula One glory.

Jarno Trulli
Less than two years ago, Jarno was still racing karts. His meteoric rise to Formula One has made a mockery of those who spend years climbing through the ranks. Despite having no family money, he attracted assistance from Benetton boss Flavio Briatore, who financed his conquest of the German Formula Three championship and placed him with Minardi.

Financial input
However, the matter of who owns Minardi has become very complicated, with Gabriele Rumi (owner of the Fondmetal Formula One team in the early 1990s) the latest to take control of some of the shares. Benetton's empire-building Flavio Briatore is in charge of the largest slice of the pie, with Minardi as a place for him to bring drivers he is considering for the future, for Benetton. This is good, as without this input, the team looked sure not to last the winter. The cash has also helped secure the services of Jarno Trulli alongside the paying Ukyo Katayama.

Last year, the team had to make do with an updated version of its 1995 chassis, but things should be better this year as there's an all-new chassis. The motivation will come from a Hart V8, this unit being picked ahead of Ford's ED4 V8 for offering better value for money.

FOR THE RECORD

Country of origin:	Italy
Team base:	Faenza, Italy
Founded:	1980
Active in Formula One:	From 1985
Grands Prix contested:	190
Grand Prix wins:	None
Pole positions:	None
Fastest laps:	None

Drivers and Results 1996

Driver	Nationality	Races	Wins	Pts	Posi
Pedro Lamy	Portuguese	16	None	None	N/A
Giancarlo Fisichella	Italian	8	None	None	N/A
Giovanni Lavaggi	Italian	6	None	None	N/A
Tarso Marques	Brazilian	2	None	None	N/A

Car specifications 1997

Team principals:	Giancarlo Minardi
Team manager:	Frederic Dhainaut
Designer:	Mauro Gennari
Chief engineer:	Gabriele Tredozi
Drivers:	Ukyo Katayama & Jarno Trulli
Test driver:	Tarso Marques
Chassis:	Minardi M197
Engine:	Hart V8
Tyres:	Bridgestone

THE TECHNICAL BRAIN: Gabriele Tredozi

STEWART

Ready, steady, go

This brand new team headed by three-time World Champion Jackie Stewart is already setting new standards in professionalism.

Jackie Stewart was effectively the first professional Formula One driver. Not because he was the first to be paid for his services, but because he was the first to embrace practices and principals that we see today as being "professional". Renowned for his meticulous approach, his new team is sure to be one of the slickest and most professional in the paddock as it strives to make its mark at motor sport's highest level.

In at the deep end

Despite claiming to have modest aims for this debut year in Formula One, the team must be hoping to at least exceed the debut performance of Jordan, the last team to make a successful impact in Formula One back in 1991. This means achieving a target of fifth place in the Constructors' Cup, which is no small undertaking.

With a chassis penned by former Footwork designer Alan Jenkins, power from Ford's best engine, tyres from Bridgestone, sponsorship from Texaco – ITV's chief backer – and fine young drivers in Rubens Barrichello and Jan Magnussen, great things could happen for Stewart Grand Prix. However, coming into Formula One gets harder every year, as even the established front-running teams are having to run to stand still in the chase after Williams.

So, it will definitely be a testing time for the tartan-clad warriors between now and the end of the season. But their arrival is more than welcome, bringing as it does the dash provided by new sponsors and the insight of one of the sport's shrewdest and most analytical brains.

FOR THE RECORD

Country of origin:	England
Team base:	Milton Keynes, England
Founded:	1987, as Paul Stewart Racing
Active in Formula One:	From 1997
Grands Prix contested:	2
Grand Prix wins:	None
Pole positions:	None
Fastest laps:	None

Car specifications 1997

Sponsors:	Texaco, Hong Kong & Shanghai Bank
President:	Jackie Stewart
Team principal:	Paul Stewart
Team manager:	Dave Stubbs
Designer:	Alan Jenkins
Drivers:	Rubens Barrichello & Jan Magnussen
Test driver:	None
Chassis:	Stewart SF1
Engine:	Ford V10
Tyres:	Bridgestone

THE DRIVERS

Rubens Barrichello

Was glad to see the back of Jordan team after five seasons that promised so much but never delivered the big prize. Will have to develop his PR skills to fit in with the corporate image of the Stewart Grand Prix team, but his on-track performances are sure to fit in very well, and his youthful speed ought to re-emerge as he applies himself.

Jan Magnussen

Another who will have to tidy up his off-track image to fit in at Stewart Grand Prix. But Jan's driving abilities could soon be the talk of the paddock. Has more natural speed than any of his contemporaries. Will now have to use his head to make this work in F1.

BIG BUSINESS: Jackie Stewart will pull every string to make his new team work

GETTING IT RIGHT

Drivers win races, cars win races, but in the ever-changing world of Formula One, tactics win races too

There's more to winning a Grand Prix than having the best car and the fastest driver, although that is obviously the best starting point. these two ingredients should normally be enough for the job in hand, ignoring freak weather or the bad luck of being caught out in a backmarker's accident.

However, what could make the difference, and it's often a small one, between success and failure, is tactics.

Since refuelling was introduced, it's no longer been a case of driving flat-out from the start, hoping everything holds together for the 200-mile race distance. While the driving is still flat-out, there are now so many more factors to consider, like whether to pit once, twice or three times, and much more besides.

Before you even get to the race itself, tactics have to be considered, such as when to set your qualifying time. You have the same as everyone else: one hour and a maximum of 12 laps. But you have to plan your attack, looking out for when the track will be clear of traffic, whether a set of tyres will produce one flying lap or can be pushed to produce two, and watching the weather forecast in case rain is due before you've done that flying lap.

When sitting on the grid, you will also have to consider the ideal number of revs to use when the five red lights go out; your best route to the first corner, tailored according to the starting abilities of those around you on the grid and making the best use of any vacant grid slots; and the 10-second stop-and-go penalty you will incur if you jump the start.

Firstly, take the planning of pit stops. Start a Grand Prix with just one planned pitstop, and your car will be full of fuel and heavier than rivals adopting a different strategy. Thus it's going to be slower off the line and harder to drive fast until the load lightens. Then, after your single stop, again you'll be driving one of the heavier cars in the race. At only two points in the race – should you last the distance – will your car be running at its lightest; on close to empty tanks.

Initially, this doesn't appear to be the cleverest plan. However, it does mean that while the others are pitting for their extra stops, you can keep going and make up places on the track. Furthermore, if the circuit has a long pitlane entry and exit – meaning it takes a long time between pulling off, chugging down the pitlane with its 75mph speed limit and then blasting off again – then this is a tactic worth considering. Also, if the circuit is like Monaco, which offers almost no overtaking places, you want to stop as few times as possible, since making up ground again could be hampered by being stuck behind slower cars. Pitting at Hockenheim isn't so costly, as it has a short pitlane and is an easy circuit for passing.

The two-stop strategy is the most popular option. However, there are races at which some of the front-running cars go for three stops,

following a practice used successfully by Michael Schumacher and Benetton in 1994. It's a risk, as you're giving the pit crew another opportunity to cross-thread one of your wheel retaining bolts, jam the fuel nozzle or any of the myriad things that can go wrong. But, if you think it will give you the slightest of margins, then you'll go for it.

There's also the consideration that on your first lap out of the pits, your new tyres won't be up to operating temperature and you'll have to take risks to lap fast, which is especially important if you know you will emerge just ahead of a rival who'd be lapping at full speed. The art of "defensive driving" would thus need to be practised... Schumacher and, to a lesser extent Jacques Villeneuve, are masters at this and waste less time than others in getting up to full speed, thus making a pitstop less of a time penalty.

Certain circuits guide your hand and force you to take more pitstops, such as the Hungaroring, which is so twisty that tyre wear is much higher than at other circuits.

Tactics can't all be decided before the race though, for many new factors can crop up once the race is underway. For example, you may have made a lousy start and lost a handful of places before the first corner. And now you're trapped behind slower cars on a circuit on which they can easily hold their line and keep you behind, letting your rivals escape.

So, you might want to bring your pitstop schedule forward and make use of an uncluttered pitlane and come out on your next set of tyres at a position in the running order whereby you have a clear track to make the most of them. Alternatively, you could wait until they've pitted then put in a handful of full-speed laps before your stop, hoping this would enable you to emerge just ahead of them. Also, you can radio the pits and ask when the neighbouring pits are going to be busy. Even waiting a second to let one pull in or pull out could blow your plans.

Finally, there is the factor of changing weather. If it's light rain, you have to decide if it will blow over and you can risk staying on slicks and hope the track will dry out. But you have to be careful when racing on a long track, such as Spa, because if you make the wrong decision you can lose a lot of time before you get back to the pits. With heavy rain, staying on slicks is out, but intermediate tyres may work, and they'll last longer than the heavily-treaded wet-weather tyres if the track starts to dry. Decisions, decisions.

WEATHER FORECASTING: Rain throws up a host of options. Do you pit for treaded tyres, or wait and see? Or is it going to be a bad day whatever you do, as your car is set up for the dry like Damon Hill's in Spain last year.

THE DRIVERS TO WATCH

Formula One can be split neatly into the haves and the have-nots. Those drivers who are part of the teams with the biggest budgets, and drive the best chassis fitted with the most powerful engines are always doing the winning. While those without the top equipment will never do much beyond playing a supporting role, until their day comes to join the big boys.

This chapter splits the drivers accordingly, looking in greatest depth at the top dozen, including the likes of Damon Hill, Michael Schumacher and Jacques Villeneuve.

However, dismiss the drivers who do battle out of the top half-dozen places – those who joust for glory and not for points – at your peril, as many of these will be the Grand Prix winners of the future. If only they can do enough to impress one of the top teams to sign them. Don't forget, when Hill made his Formula One debut in 1992, it was with the fading Brabham team and he was able to qualify just twice in eight attempts.

Four years later, as a Williams driver, he was crowned World Champion.

In 1996 the finishing order was Hill, Villeneuve, Schumacher, Jean Alesi, Mika Hakkinen, Gerhard Berger and David Coulthard, but don't expect a repeat performance this season, even though all but Hill have stayed with the same teams. For starters, if Heinz-Harald Frentzen is as good as Frank Williams thinks he is, good enough to replace Hill at Williams, he ought to have the title in his pocket with several rounds to go. But, of course Villeneuve came close in 1996, in his first season of Formula One, so he will keep Frentzen alert and may even beat him.

However, one of the other teams could always pull a blinder and build a chassis over the winter that trumps the others. But, a glance at the Williams team's amazing run of success in the past decade suggests that they are unlikely to be toppled, especially as Adrian Newey is still running the design side and Renault's engines will be as strong as ever.

Expect Ferrari's Schumacher and Eddie Irvine, both of whom were hampered by the team's design quandary last year, to be at the front more often. After all, this is the year Schumacher predicted he would win his third world title. Benetton's Alesi and Berger will be as fast, wild and woolly as before. But, look

this year to Hakkinen and Coulthard winning for McLaren. After all, Mercedes expects it.

So, that's the big four teams, but watch drivers such as Johnny Herbert at Sauber, Olivier Panis at Ligier, Mika Salo at Tyrrell, Jan Magnussen at the new Stewart Grand Prix team or newcomer Ralf Schumacher at Jordan, for they are all likely to pop up in the points from time to time.

Finally, just remember, whenever you think from the comfort of your armchair that you could do a better job than some of the "tail-end Charlies", that no-one on a Grand Prix grid is a fool. It's just that some of them appear to behave that way from time to time...

THE CLASS OF 1997: Back row: E. Irvine, R. Barrichello, J. Magnussen, D. Coulthard, M. Hakkinen, R. Schumacher, G. Fisichella, R. Rosset and V. Sospiri. **Middle row:** M. Schumacher, J. Trulli, U. Katayama, J. Villeneuve, H.H. Frentzen, S. Nakano and O. Panis. **Front row:** J. Verstappen, M. Salo, P. Diniz, D. Hill, N. Larini, J. Herbert, G. Berger and J. Alesi.

JEAN ALESI

The great entertainer

Jean Alesi is exactly how Hollywood would cast a Formula One driver. He's dark in looks, Latin in temperament and very fast. The fans love him, but his emotions still trip him up.

Jean Alesi is going to have to grow up a great deal in 1997 if he is to keep his drive through until 1998. That's the message from Flavio Briatore, his boss at Benetton, who came close to releasing him from his contract at the end of last year as he was upset with Jean for letting his emotions rule rather than his brain.

In fact, Jean came very close to being cast out of the team several times last year when he appeared to favour outright speed and maximum drama to bringing home the points. Yes, he crashed out of the first race in Australia when in the points, and did so again three races later at the European Grand Prix when impatient to atone for a bad start. Then he wrecked his car exiting the first corner on the first lap of the season's closing race in Japan.

However, between these lapses, Jean was the more consistent of the Benetton drivers, scoring points in each of the 11 races he finished. Indeed, Jean was second on no fewer than four occasions, so he can't be all bad. And, without doubt, he is still the most spectacular driver to watch, particularly when track conditions are damp or wet.

For all this speed though, Jean has but one win (in the 1995 Canadian Grand Prix) for all his efforts after 118 Grands Prix. And, apart from his early days at Tyrrell, he's usually been in one of the best cars. So you have to wonder if Jean has the mental agility to read a race to full effect and turn a good drive into a winning one.

A big hit in Italy

To the fanatical Italian *tifosi*, Jean should be forgiven his misdemeanours, for he *was*

Ferrari. He may have scored just one win during his five seasons there, but he echoed the passion and the perpetual glorious failure of this mighty team. They adored him so much that they ignored the fact that he raced as a Frenchman. What mattered to them was that his bloodline was Italian, from Sardinia. Equally, his heart was with the marque of the prancing horse, Ferrari. And he had their temperament, fiery and passionate, in tune with the ups and the downs of the team if not ideal for helping sort these oscillations.

But that came to an end when he moved lock, stock and barrel from Ferrari to Benetton with team-mate Gerhard Berger for 1996. Life was different at Benetton. Although the team is owned by the Benetton family and run by Briatore, it's based in Britain and crewed by a British workforce. So, outbursts of Latin temperament are not seen as the way forward. And it was here that conflict occurred, with Briatore making noises early in the year that he wouldn't tolerate Jean's rages and hot-headed moments. If Berger could behave rationally, why couldn't Jean? Then, just before it came to a head, Jean calmed down and the results started to come. Although when Jean threw his car off on the opening lap in Japan, it cost Benetton second position in the Constructors' Cup, and caused Briatore to lose his rag again.

But what made Briatore sign him in the first place, apart from his following in Italy, which was obviously important to Benetton as it has jumpers to sell? His past, that's what. For Jean was a hotshot in French Formula Renault and French Formula Three in the mid-1980s, he

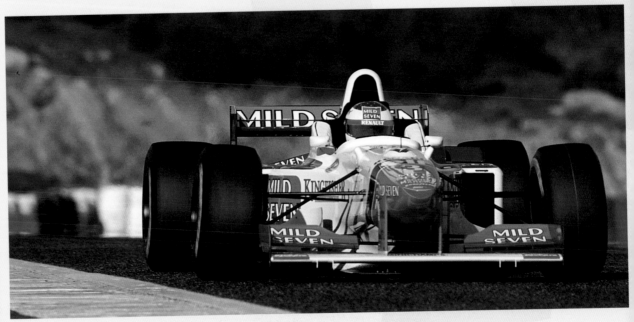

HIGH ON EMOTION: Jean Alesi was always fast for Benetton in 1996, but too wild, too often

was Formula 3000 Champion for Eddie Jordan Racing in 1989, also making a stunning debut for Tyrrell in that year's French Grand Prix, finishing fourth. And, then of course there was that audacious move when Senna passed him in the first race of 1990, at Phoenix, and Jean passed him back.

A star in the wet

No one is better than Jean in mixed conditions: when it comes to car control in extremis, even Schumacher is left trailing, as shown at the Nurburgring back in 1995. Mind you, he's not bad in torrential conditions either, as shown at Barcelona last year when he was best of the rest behind an even more inspired than usual Schumacher.

So, will the Benetton team try to make Jean feel loved to encourage the best out of him in 1997 and enable him to calm down sufficiently to use all that the race-winning Renault V10 can produce? Or will it all come to a head the next time he takes one risk too many and throws away a points-scoring position? Wait and see…

> " *I always do things to my maximum.* "
> JEAN ALESI

TRACK NOTES

Nationality: . . . . FRENCH
Born: . . . . 11 JUNE, 1964,
. . . . AVIGNON, FRANCE
Teams: . . . . . . TYRRELL 1989–90,
FERRARI 1991–95, BENETTON 1996–97

Career record

First Grand Prix start: . 1989 FRANCE
Grand Prix starts: 120
Grand Prix wins: 1
1995 . . . . *Canada*
Poles: 1
Fastest laps: 4
Points: 190
Honours: . . . 1989 FORMULA 3000
CHAMPION, 1987 FRENCH FORMULA
THREE CHAMPION

HOTTEST DRIVE: US GP 1990 when he diced for lead with Ayrton Senna's McLaren
BIGGEST SETBACK: His Ferrari retiring from the lead near the end of the 1995 Italian GP
MOST LIKELY TO SAY: "I need people around me to want me to win."
LEAST LIKELY TO SAY: "It's impossible to drive sideways."

MORE WINS NEEDED: Jean Alesi will have to start winning for Benetton in 1997 or he will be looking for a new ride

GERHARD BERGER

The unlikely statesman

ALWAYS MR NICE GUY: Gerhard Berger has a tendency to make friends like few others in the combative world of Formula One

Gerhard Berger never expected to become the elder statesman of Formula One. But now the practical joker of yesteryear is just that: Mr Dependable. Still extremely fast, no one discounts him.

From the moment he arrived in Formula One, Gerhard Berger was a breath of fresh air. He was quick, but he was also game for a laugh whenever the opportunity arose and lightened the often stuffy atmosphere in the paddock. He even did the unimaginable and made his team-mate Ayrton Senna take life less seriously.

If it hadn't been for Senna, though, Gerhard would have more than nine Grand Prix wins to his tally after the near 200 Grands Prix in which he's competed since his debut with the little ATS team back at the end of 1984. For when he and Senna were team-mates at McLaren between 1990 and 1992, the affable Austrian was very much the number two driver. And, although Gerhard was runner-up behind the great Brazilian just twice during that period, he was also second in five other races and you get the feeling that if the team hadn't been so focused on Senna, then some of those drives could easily have become wins.

Many drivers can say "if only", but this lanky individual has perhaps more call than most in this department. If anything, the only people who don't underestimate Berger are the sport's insiders. For they have witnessed his speed and know he would have won more often if he hadn't been at Ferrari when the team was in disarray from 1993 to 1995 and they notice that it was Berger as opposed to his more flamboyant team-mate Jean Alesi who was the faster Benetton driver in the second half of 1996.

A poor start to the year

Gerhard himself was down on power for the first half of 1996, suffering from the tail end of pneumonia. But then as his health returned, bad luck started to dog him, and Alesi ended up

Racing is more than just going quick through a corner. It's the whole package.
GERHARD BERGER

with the larger points tally come season's end.

Memories in Formula One are short and people only remember winners. For example, do you remember who won last year's German Grand Prix? Why, Damon Hill of course. But who led it until three laps from the end before his engine blew? Berger, and Alesi was well over 15 seconds behind at the time. Then, while Hill was streaking off alone at the start of the Japanese Grand Prix, who was it who stuck with him and then nearly took him off? Berger, proving that although he is 37, he's still one of the fastest out there.

However, although not taking rash driving manoeuvres quite to the degree that Alesi does, his pair of attacks on Eddie Irvine's Ferrari at Estoril and then Suzuka raise the question that perhaps now he needs glasses. And not just for reading…

Still, it has been a very long time since Gerhard arrived in Formula One. And it must seem light-years ago when he started racing, in an Alfasud, back in 1981.

Formula Three followed and Gerhard Berger was a star in the European Championship in 1984, graduating to Formula One midway through that year.

Full speed ahead

So, what hope does he have for 1997? Pretty good, as he's fully settled in at Benetton and has a character that is more in tune with a British workforce than is Alesi's, which is why this time around he will be seen within the Benetton camp as the number one driver, an honour that was initially bestowed on Alesi last year. And, for 1997, he will be racing with a car that has been designed to fit his tall frame and be driven the way he likes.

Last year's car was very much a Schumacher legacy, set up to be very nervous – just how the German likes it – but was certainly not to the liking of either Berger or Alesi. And Gerhard spent most of his early test outings crashing the thing.

If the results don't come his way in the season ahead, perhaps it will be time for Gerhard to step aside and let some of the younger drivers have a go. And he needn't worry about being left penniless in retirement, for despite negotiating all his own retainers with the teams, Gerhard has long been one of the best paid drivers. It will simply be a matter of whether he wants to be near the sea for sailing or the mountains for skiing…

TRACK NOTES

Nationality:	AUSTRIAN
Born:	27 AUGUST, 1959,
	WORGL, AUSTRIA
Teams:	ATS 1984, ARROWS 1985,
	BENETTON 1986,
	FERRARI 1987–1989,
	McLAREN 1990–1992,
	FERRARI 1993–1995,
	BENETTON 1996–1997

Career record

First Grand Prix start:	1984 AUSTRIA
Grand Prix starts:	198
Grand Prix wins:	9
1986	Mexico
1987	Japan, Australia
1988	Italy
1989	Portugal
1991	Japan
1992	Canada, Australia
1994	Germany
Poles:	11
Fastest laps:	19
Points:	367
Honours:	1988 & 1994 THIRD IN WORLD CHAMPIONSHIPS, 1984 MONACO FORMULA THREE RUNNER-UP

HOTTEST DRIVE: Winning 1988 Italian GP for Ferrari, just four weeks after Enzo Ferrari died
BIGGEST SETBACK: Burning hands in fiery shunt at Imola in 1989
MOST LIKELY TO SAY: "I didn't mean to run into your car Eddie (Irvine)."
LEAST LIKELY TO SAY: "Last year's Benetton fitted me like a glove."

HEADING FOR POINTS: Fourth place in France signalled the beginning of an upturn for Gerhard Berger in last season's Formula One championship

DAVID COULTHARD

Best of the British

Having broken into Formula One with the dominant Williams team and won a Grand Prix, moving to McLaren meant wins were off the agenda in 1996. But this young Scot is a class act and could strike again this season.

Driving for McLaren, David Coulthard is poised this season to become Britain's top Formula One driver, for he is more than likely to outpace former Williams team-mate Damon Hill now that Hill has headed for Arrows. And this will be somewhat sweet for David, because Hill starts the season as Formula One World Champion and David does not. Yet, had David played his cards right and kept his Williams ride, he could have been.

This may sound confusing, but, put simply, it all boils down to Hill driving for the all-conquering Williams team in 1996, while David transferred from Williams across to McLaren. While the former team won 12 of last year's 16 Grands Prix, McLaren won none. David left a winning team for one that didn't, and all because he'd previously entered into an agreement with McLaren and had to honour it at a time when the bosses at Williams were more inclined to run the Scotsman, rather than the Englishman, alongside Jacques Villeneuve in last year's line-up. There are a few "if onlys" in this argument, but had David stayed at Williams he would surely have ended up higher than the seventh place overall he managed for McLaren.

Handling problems

However, that's water under the bridge, and David is looking forward to 1997 with renewed excitement, confident that the handling peculiarities of last year's McLaren have been sorted to his liking. Which they certainly were not in 1996, with David at sea in the opening three races when he couldn't get close to team-mate Mika Hakkinen. Then, just as he became confident with the car – he led for the first 19 laps in the fourth race, the San Marino Grand Prix at Imola, and then chased Olivier Panis home to finish second at Monaco next time out – the team followed Hakkinen's advice and opted for a short wheelbase version from mid-season on, which Coulthard didn't like at all. Jackie Stewart is one of many who consider David is quick only when he has

A SERIOUS CHALLENGER: David Coulthard expects to win races in his second year with McLaren

a car that is completely to his liking, and is somewhat off the pace when he doesn't. A glance at last year's results tends to support that. There certainly were times when he was less than happy with the way the car behaved, and he failed to score in the final five races, enabling Hakkinen to overtake David in the championship standings.

On the plus side, the power offered by the Mercedes engines used by McLaren was never in doubt, and David recorded the fastest straight line speed of the year, when he was clocked at a whisker under 222mph on one of the long straights at Hockenheim.

However, the chassis was never really sorted to make the most of this, and it really couldn't cope when the circuit was a mix of mid- and low-speed corners.

Their chances for 1997 are far brighter, and providing they manage not to take each other off as at Estoril last year, the battle between David and Hakkinen should be gripping. Whether they will be in line to win races remains to be seen, but a top team like McLaren has bounced back from the doldrums before and will do so again.

An excellent pedigree

Encouraged into racing karts from the age of eight by his kart-racing father Duncan, David hit the ground running when he moved to cars in 1989. In fact, he so impressed in Formula Ford that McLaren and *Autosport* (motor racing's weekly must-read magazine) launched a scholarship award. His prize was a run in a McLaren. His Formula Vauxhall season with Paul Stewart Racing was interrupted by a leg-breaking shunt in 1990, but David bounced back and finished as runner-up to Rubens Barrichello in the 1991 British Formula Three Championship, going on to win the prestigious Formula Three race around the streets of Macau in the Far East. Then the money ran out, and despite winning once in Formula 3000 all momentum looked lost as he accepted a test driver's role at Williams for 1994. But Ayrton Senna's death propelled David into the big time and he has never looked back.

Coulthard put the trials and tribulations of 1996 behind him from the very start of the 1997 season. From fourth on the grid, and always near the front, he stormed through to win the Australian Grand Prix by 20 seconds.

> *Inevitably I still make mistakes, but that's how you learn.*
>
> DAVID COULTHARD

NOT A FLYING START: David Coulthard struggled in his first few outings for McLaren, but got moving by the fourth Grand Prix

TRACK NOTES

Nationality: . . . . SCOTTISH
Born: . . . . 27 MARCH, 1971,
. . . . TWYNHOLM, SCOTLAND
Teams: . . . . WILLIAMS 1994–95,
. . . . McLAREN 1996–1997

Career record

First Grand Prix start: . . . 1994 SPAIN
Grand Prix starts: 43
Grand Prix wins: 2
   1995 . . . . *Portugal*
   1997 . . . . *Australia*
Poles: 5
Fastest laps: 4
Points: 91
Honours: . 1991 BRITISH FORMULA THREE RUNNER-UP & MACAU GP WINNER, 1989 McLAREN AUTOSPORT YOUNG DRIVER OF THE YEAR, 1988 SCOTTISH KART CHAMPION

HOTTEST DRIVE: Leading 1996 San Marino GP in unfancied McLaren
BIGGEST SETBACK: Being affected by tonsillitis through first half of 1995
MOST LIKELY TO SAY: "You've got to stay level-headed."
LEAST LIKELY TO SAY: "I made a really bad start."

HEINZ-HARALD FRENTZEN

In from the cold

FIRST TASTE: Heinz-Harald Frentzen gets to grips with a Williams for the first time at Estoril late last year

It is going to take Frentzen a long time to be thought of as anything other than the man without spectacular results who took Hill's ride at Williams. Watch him though, for he's a flier.

Formula One fans could be given a very clear example in 1997 of the difference between a top team and one that hangs around in the middle of a Grand Prix grid. For Damon Hill has headed to join the TWR Arrows team as a direct result of Heinz-Harald Frentzen heading the opposite way, having been picked from the relative anonymity of a Sauber ride to take Hill's place at the dominant Williams team.

If, as most expect, Frentzen gets immediately on to the ultimate pace, leading the way from the first Grand Prix of this season with Williams team-mate Jacques Villeneuve, while Hill struggles mid-grid at Arrows, the matter will be exposed for good. The fact is that any of the top dozen drivers could win a Grand Prix if allowed a shot in the best car, which has

been the Williams-Renault for the past handful of seasons. Listen to Eddie Irvine expostulate on the subject, and you will be left in no uncertainty that this is the case, and that his 1996 Ferrari was not really a winning car, except in the hands of the extraordinary Michael Schumacher. While Damon Hill and Jacques Villeneuve on the other hand…

Quicker than Schumacher?

Talk to Formula One insiders, though, and few feel that Frentzen will be exposed as a fraud and fail to win races for Williams. For many have had the hunch for several years that Frentzen is also a little bit special. Quicker, whisper it, even than Schumacher, a compatriot who not only got all the breaks

to leap into Formula One ahead of Frentzen, but also pinched his girlfriend, now Schumacher's wife Corinna.

Naturally very fast in everything he's raced, but with a history of using his right foot rather more than his head, the 1997 season will also reveal whether Heinz-Harald can test and develop a car as well as he can race one. And the Williams team will be able to see just how good Hill was at developing a car, and how much Villeneuve learnt from him.

Many felt that Heinz-Harald didn't give it everything at Sauber through the 1996 season, especially when he knew that his Ford-powered car was not as competitive as it had been in 1995 when he managed to guide it home third at Monza. Also, with his name allegedly already on a Williams contract, many felt that he was just biding his time, anxious not to take any unnecessary risks. But Heinz-Harald will fiercely deny this and tell you that he had his Sauber cranked up pretty well to qualify it seventh in the season-closing race in Japan.

It also must be pointed out that a lack of effort on his half would be unlikely, as he viewed the Sauber team like a family and even stood by them, turning down the chance to jump ship to Williams in 1994 after Ayrton Senna's death, because team-mate Karl Wendlinger was injured at the following Grand Prix at Monaco, and he wouldn't countenance leaving Sauber in the lurch.

Heinz-Harald, like almost all of his contemporaries, raced karts successfully. Formula Ford 2000 followed and he was runner-up in the German Championship back in

1987. He went one better the following year and won the inaugural German Formula Opel series, taking time out at the end of the year to win the final two European Championship races ahead of a driver by the name of Mika Hakkinen.

Runner-up to Wendlinger in the 1989 German Formula Three Championship, Heinz-Harald moved on to Formula 3000, but he was also offered a Mercedes sportscar drive, which he soon turned down to concentrate on his single-seater career. Success in Formula 3000 didn't come though, and after two years he

headed to Japan for 1992 and 1993 where he was an occasional winner before being summoned in 1994 to Formula One by Sauber, who fittingly used Mercedes engines. And, ever since, the speed has been there for all to see.

**"*From now on, everything changes for me.*
HEINZ-HARALD FRENTZEN "**

TRACK NOTES

Nationality: .... GERMAN
Born: .... 18 MAY, 1967,
. MÖNCHENGLADBACH, GERMANY
Teams: ...... SAUBER 1994–1996,
.... WILLIAMS 1997

Career record

First Grand Prix start: . .1994 BRAZIL
Grand Prix starts: 50
Grand Prix wins: .... None
.... *(best result: third,*
.... *1995 Italy)*
Poles: .... None
Fastest laps: 1
Points: 29
Honours: 1989 GERMAN FORMULA THREE RUNNER-UP, 1988 GERMAN FORMULA OPEL CHAMPION, 1984 GERMAN JUNIOR KARTING CHAMPION

HOTTEST DRIVE: Qualifying fifth for his Grand Prix debut in Brazil in 1994.
BIGGEST SETBACK: Choosing to turn back on Mercedes sportscar and go F3000, with team-mate Schumacher getting F1 break within that year.
MOST LIKELY TO SAY: "Sauber gave me the opportunity to show my potential."
LEAST LIKELY TO SAY: "Michael Schumacher is my best friend."

THE BIG CHANCE: His apprenticeship served, Heinz-Harald Frentzen is now armed with the best car in Formula One, the Williams-Renault FW18. And must win

MIKA HAKKINEN

Ready and waiting

Mika Hakkinen should have been a Grand Prix winner a long time ago — he came to Formula One with a fabulous pedigree — but still he hasn't found the car in which to claim that first win.

Before Mika Hakkinen graduated to Formula One, he was better than Michael Schumacher. Better than any driver his Formula Three team boss Dick Bennetts had seen since former charge Ayrton Senna. And Mika was equally capable of making the huge jump straight to Formula One from Formula Three and to run on the pace immediately. Yet, amazingly, poised to start his seventh season of Formula One, Mika still hasn't got off the mark. He's done 79 Grands Prix prior to the start of this season and still not broken his duck, scored his first win. Three times he's brought his car home second, but never first.

MR McLAREN: Mika Hakkinen – at McLaren since 1993 and still chasing a win. Chasing hard

Championships galore

Starting in karts at the age of six, Mika was five-times Finnish Champion before he moved up to Formula Ford in 1987, gunning to try and do as well as fellow Finn JJ Lehto had done the year before. In fact, Mika did even better and won a clean sweep of the Finnish, Swedish and Nordic titles. Formula Opel followed and he was European Champion in that.
Formula Three took two years to crack, but he won the 1990 British title after a season-long scrap with compatriot Mika Salo, as well as

winning other races around Europe and the Macau Formula Three Grand Prix, turning himself into a really hot property.
Lotus snatched him up for the 1991 Formula One season and he showed immediate pace, despite his steering wheel coming off in his hands on his debut at Phoenix.

Sure there have been setbacks along the way, such as not getting to compete in a race in 1993 until the final three rounds after a gamble to leave the struggling Lotus team and join McLaren went wrong. Senna decided not to retire after all and Mika found himself the third driver in a two-car team behind Senna and Indycar convert Michael Andretti. Only when Andretti was forced to accept that his Formula One dream was not working and headed back Stateside did Mika get the nod and stepped forward from the McLaren test team. He out-qualified Senna in Portugal, to show that he had lost none of his flair while sitting on the sidelines.

Mika's darkest day

Then there was the terrible accident that threatened his life after an incident in qualifying for the 1995 Australian Grand Prix. A tyre deflated suddenly and he was a passenger, as his McLaren snapped out of control on the entry to a corner and slammed sideways into a tyre barrier at over 100mph. However, Mika remains unflappable and after a winter of convalescence he bounced back from the head injury, convinced that his first Grand Prix win will come when the time is right. And, in fairness to Mika,

LOOKING TO THE FUTURE: Mika Hakkinen starts 1997 with his best chance of success

TRACK NOTES

Nationality: . . . . FINNISH
Born: . . . . . . 28 SEPTEMBER, 1968,
. . . . HELSINKI, FINLAND
Teams: . . . . . . LOTUS 1991–1992,
. . . . McLAREN 1993–1997

Career record
First Grand Prix start: . . 1991 UNITED
. . . . .STATES
Grand Prix starts: 81
Grand Prix wins: . . . . None
. . . (best results: second, 1994
Belgium; 1995 Italy, Japan)
Poles: . . . . None
Fastest laps: . . . . None
Points: 98
Honours: . 1990 BRITISH FORMULA
THREE CHAMPION, 1988 EUROPEAN
FORMULA OPEL CHAMPION, 1987
SCANDINAVIAN FORMULA FORD
CHAMPION, 1986 FINNISH
KARTING CHAMPION

HOTTEST DRIVE: Out-qualified Ayrton Senna at Estoril in 1993, in their first race as McLaren team-mates
BIGGEST SETBACK: Life-threatening accident in 1995 Australian GP
MOST LIKELY TO SAY: "The McLaren is not yet as fast as the Williams."
LEAST LIKELY TO SAY: "I never think about my accident in Adelaide."

> *When I get the (winning) car, I'm ready to win.*
>
> MIKA HAKKINEN

it never has yet, although matters did look promising in last year's Belgian Grand Prix, until the Safety Car came out while the wreckage from Jos Verstappen's accident was cleared. This meant Mika and McLaren's correct guess of fuel strategy was blown, rendered *hors de combat*.

Mika also felt that he could have been in with a shot at victory in the Italian Grand Prix when he suffered from having to make an unscheduled pitstop for a new nosecone on only the fourth lap of the race. Jean Alesi had clipped one of the unpopular stacks of tyres

that had been specially positioned at the chicanes and threw them back into Mika's path. Mika's recovery – to third place – showed what sort of result could have been gained without this mishap, especially as he had been lying third at the time of the incident.

Many have said that Mika is too wild and undisciplined to make that final step to Grand Prix glory. But don't you believe it. This may have been true in the past, with immaturity and desperation making him over-drive in an attempt to keep up and make several mistakes in 1995. But that was then and this is now.

Equally, that was before his Adelaide 1995 accident, and Mika has had time enough to think about things and put them into perspective since, to go for a win when the machinery at hand is capable of it, and to go for points when it's not.

JOHNNY HERBERT

Go Johnny, go!

Formula One is no longer a laughing matter for Johnny Herbert, as this season he is number one at Sauber and deadly serious about becoming a regular points scorer for the Swiss team.

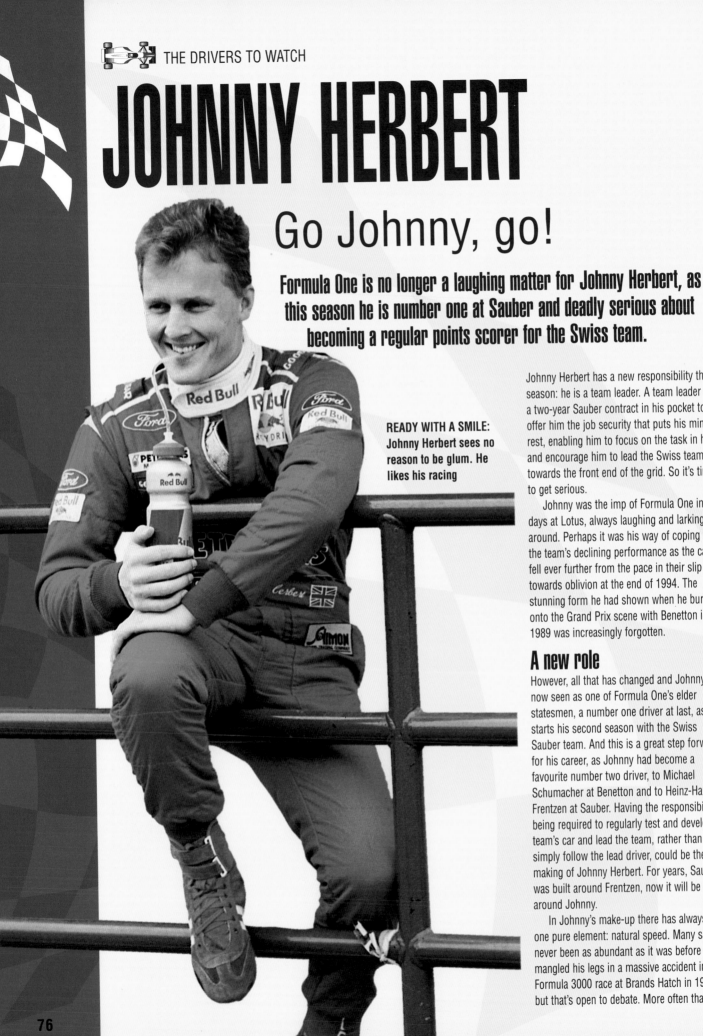

READY WITH A SMILE: Johnny Herbert sees no reason to be glum. He likes his racing

Johnny Herbert has a new responsibility this season: he is a team leader. A team leader with a two-year Sauber contract in his pocket to offer him the job security that puts his mind at rest, enabling him to focus on the task in hand and encourage him to lead the Swiss team towards the front end of the grid. So it's time to get serious.

Johnny was the imp of Formula One in his days at Lotus, always laughing and larking around. Perhaps it was his way of coping with the team's declining performance as the cars fell ever further from the pace in their slip towards oblivion at the end of 1994. The stunning form he had shown when he burst onto the Grand Prix scene with Benetton in 1989 was increasingly forgotten.

A new role

However, all that has changed and Johnny is now seen as one of Formula One's elder statesmen, a number one driver at last, as he starts his second season with the Swiss Sauber team. And this is a great step forward for his career, as Johnny had become a favourite number two driver, to Michael Schumacher at Benetton and to Heinz-Harald Frentzen at Sauber. Having the responsibility of being required to regularly test and develop the team's car and lead the team, rather than simply follow the lead driver, could be the making of Johnny Herbert. For years, Sauber was built around Frentzen, now it will be built around Johnny.

In Johnny's make-up there has always been one pure element: natural speed. Many say it's never been as abundant as it was before he mangled his legs in a massive accident in a Formula 3000 race at Brands Hatch in 1988, but that's open to debate. More often than not, if Johnny hasn't been up at the front tussling over the lead, it's simply been a case of being at the wheel of the number two car, which means getting all the development tweaks after the number one driver and being given comparatively little testing.

Don't forget, Johnny was still able to pick up Grand Prix wins in 1995 in both Britain and Italy for Benetton, admittedly both times benefiting from Hill having knocked Schumacher off the track. However, he also scored only three points less than Frentzen last year, gaining on his team leader's pace with every race and occasionally outpacing him in the races in the latter half of the year. And this performance was recognised when he was promoted to team leader for 1997 on Frentzen's departure to Williams.

Speed to burn

From the outset of Johnny's career it was clear to see that he was something special. The cheeky chappy from Romford had no silver spoon in his mouth, but he had speed to burn. Hot from a golden karting career that included two British titles, he made a strong impact in Formula Ford, winning the famous Formula Ford Festival at Brands Hatch in 1985 in a field that included Damon Hill. Money became a problem, but Eddie Jordan signed him for his Formula 3 team in 1987 and Johnny rewarded him with the British title, again beating Hill.

Then came Formula 3000, again with Eddie

Jordan. He made an instant impact by winning the opening round, but his year and almost his career were cut short by a violent accident at Brands Hatch that ripped the front end off his car and left Johnny with serious foot injuries. Ironically, that very morning he had signed to drive for Benetton for the following year.

After a winter of intensive physiotherapy, Johnny made it, wowing the entire Formula One pitlane by finishing a very competitive fourth first time out in Brazil, just 10 seconds behind race winner Nigel Mansell. However, it soon became clear on the twistier tracks that Johnny's injuries were not fully healed – he couldn't brake to full effect – so he was dropped.

A period of occasional Formula One drives with Tyrrell and Lotus and a season in Japanese Formula 3000 followed, but Lotus picked him up full-time for 1991 and his career was back on the rails, albeit hampered as Lotus ran increasingly short of money, and thus the development required to stay at the front in Formula One.

> ## "
> ### Sauber has been very good and fair with me.
> #### JOHNNY HERBERT "

OVER THE KERBS: Herbert never stopped trying for Sauber in 1996 and is now team leader

TRACK NOTES

Nationality: . . . . ENGLISH
Born: . . . . 27 JUNE, 1964,
. . . . ROMFORD, ENGLAND
Teams: . . . . BENETTON 1989,
TYRRELL 1989, LOTUS 1990–1994,
LIGIER 1994, BENETTON 1994–1995,
SAUBER 1996–1997

Career record

First Grand Prix start: . . 1989 BRAZIL
Grand Prix starts: 98
Grand Prix wins: 2
1995 . . . . *Britian, Italy*
Poles: . . . . None
Fastest laps: . . . . None
Points: 67
Honours: 1991 LE MANS 24 HOURS
WINNER, 1987 BRITISH FORMULA
THREE CHAMPION, 1985 FORMULA
FORD FESTIVAL WINNER

HOTTEST DRIVE: Finishing fourth on his Formula One debut.
BIGGEST SETBACK: Leg-shattering shunt in Formula 3000 in 1988.
MOST LIKELY TO SAY: "People don't treat me seriously because I don't go around with a long face."
LEAST LIKELY TO SAY: "There's no place for humour in Formula One."

DAMON HILL

No more Mr Nice Guy

They said he wasn't quick enough, or self-centred enough to become Formula One World Champion. But Damon Hill spent a winter toughening up both physically and mentally and his new-found mettle paid dividends in 1996.

It's two-one to Michael Schumacher, and this season Damon Hill would love to get even, but following his shock move to the TWR Arrows team this is highly unlikely, no matter how well he drives nor how well Tom Walkinshaw's restructured team performs this season.

Damon has got the momentum and the World Championship, and he loves the taste of victory. But despite the fact that Damon simply gets better with every season, there will have to be a quantum leap in terms of performance from the ingredients he will be armed with in 1997. Namely, the Arrows chassis and the Yamaha engine. However, the use of

Bridgestone tyres, which are new to Formula One, could prove to be a secret weapon that will help the team move onto a new plane of competitiveness. Whether this will mean going from the tail-end of the grid to the midfield or even to the rear of the points-scoring group will remain to be seen.

The mental battle

The merest mention of Schumacher's name used to pitch Damon into a state of unrest, causing his eyebrows to knit and his dark eyes to fix on a distant target. But not now, for in 1996 Damon did more than get tough, he got

even. He performed with such conviction that Schumacher became a support act. After two seasons of being told he should be beating Schumacher because his Williams-Renault was better than the Benetton, and not being able to do so enough to land the title, Damon was brow-beaten. His many critics had crowed in 1995 when Damon triggered a number of accidents as he collided with Schumacher. Lovely bloke they said, but he can't beat a slower car, and definitely can't overtake. It's terrible how jealous people can be. If you come into any sport as the son of a famous father, people in every dark corner can't wait for you to fall on your face. However well you go, there will always be charges of nepotism and the critics will carp from behind their blinkers.

Luckily, Damon kicked off last year man enough to take it on the chin and to land the one thing that would satisfy them that he was more than just a famous name. He had to become World Champion, a feat his father Graham managed twice in the 1960s.

Making push-ups pay

Damon had spent the winter training as never before and he wasn't going to have sand kicked in his face any more. Not only was he mentally sorted and fully focused on the most important task in his life – to become World Champion – but he was coiled like a spring, physically tuned to perfection. In a world of ultimate performance, the driver had become

TYRE TESTING: Damon Hill was delighted with Bridgestone's rubber on his first acquaintance at Suzuka last year

ALL SMILES: Damon Hill showed his teeth in 1996, and not just when he was smiling

TRACK NOTES

Nationality: . . . . ENGLISH
Born: . . . . . . SEPTEMBER 17, 1960,
. . . . HAMPSTEAD, LONDON
Teams: . . . . BRABHAM 1992,
WILLIAMS 1993–96, ARROWS 1997

Career record

First Grand Prix start: . 1992 BRITAIN
Grand Prix starts: 68
Grand Prix wins: 21
   1993 . . . . *Hungary, Belgium, Italy*
   1994 . . . .*Spain, Britain, Belgium,*
   . . . . *Italy, Portugal, Japan*
   1995 . . . . *Argentina, San Marino,*
   . . . . *Hungary, Australia*
   1996 . . . . *Australia, Brazil,*
   . .*Argentina, San Marino, Canada,*
   . . . . . . *France, Germany, Japan*
Poles: 20
Fastest laps: 19
Points: 326
Honours: . . WORLD CHAMPION 1996

HOTTEST DRIVE: 1994 Japanese GP in torrential rain at Suzuka to take title race with Schumacher down to the final round in Australia.
BIGGEST SETBACK: Being knocked into a wall by Schumacher in 1994 Adelaide finale.
MOST LIKELY TO SAY: "If only I'd made a better start…"
LEAST LIKELY TO SAY: "Frank Williams gave me plenty of warning before he fired me."

the least developed part of the package. And super-fit Schumacher had previously been the only driver to truly tackle this problem. Others would not only fade as the race wore on, but also let their concentration waver. A hundredth of a second here, a tenth there, and they were underachieving. And so Damon erased this disadvantage, weakening Schumacher's hand.

To make matters even more in Damon's favour, Michael had followed Formula One's biggest ever pay cheque to Ferrari, a less competitive package than his Benetton of old. Despite claiming 1996 was for learning and 1997 for a serious title bid, he expected to be nipping at Damon's tail, winding him up as ever before. Yet, the Ferrari wasn't up to it and Damon was simply out of reach. Four wins from the first five races established who was boss. And it was Damon's Williams team mate Jacques Villeneuve who pushed him all the way to the final round, not Schumacher,

although the German did notch up three race wins all the same.

Damon's early days in racing were not so glorious, as he was propelled direct from a brief two-wheeled racing career into Formula Ford 2000. There he was put in against much more experienced drivers under the full glare of the media spotlight. There was hardly a corner he didn't spin at that day back in 1984, and he was miles off the pace. Damon was not a quitter back then either and he re-emerged in 1985 to prove himself a frontrunner in the less powerful Formula Ford 1600. Three seasons of Formula Three followed, with four wins and second place in the 1988 Formula Three Macau GP. Hampered by a lack of cash, he struggled to land a worthwhile Formula 3000 drive, although he shone brightly enough when leading on numerous occasions for the Middlebridge team to land a Williams test driving berth. And the rest you know…

 Winning the World Championship is a wonderful release of pressure.
DAMON HILL

EDDIE IRVINE

Ferrari's crazy horse

He behaved impeccably last season as Michael Schumacher's number two at Ferrari and is now poised to pose a threat after a winter of testing and development work.

Famed as Formula One's rebel, Eddie Irvine joined the establishment in 1996. His first season with Ferrari was far from being a dream one, and he did well to generally button his lip when Ferrari was in the mire in mid-season. However, he subsequently told it like it was, being all but denied any testing as team-mate Michael Schumacher was entrusted with revising the car so that it would work, even finish races. But Eddie stayed within the bounds of constructive criticism and didn't put a foot out of line. He even had just cause to

berate Formula One's elder statesman Gerhard Berger for colliding with him in both of the last two Grands Prix, in Portugal and Japan. The late Ayrton Senna, who saw fit to punch Eddie after the Ulsterman's first Grand Prix, would chuckle at the thought of it…

A long apprenticeship

Eddie served a long apprenticeship, first at home in his native Northern Ireland and then in England, winning the British Formula Ford title and the Festival in 1987. A front-runner but

never a race winner in Formula Three, Eddie convinced the right people of his talents and moved on to Formula 3000 in 1989. In 1990, when driving for Eddie Jordan Racing, he ended the season third overall, ahead of Damon Hill, Heinz-Harald Frentzen and Karl Wendlinger among others.

With no Formula One rides up for grabs, he packed his bags and trod the increasingly well-worn route to the Far East, where he raced in Japanese Formula 3000 for three seasons, winding up as runner-up in 1993. It was at the end of this last season that he was given his Formula One break by Jordan at the Suzuka circuit he had come to know so well. So well, that he was able to pull off a move on Senna that provoked the punch mentioned earlier.

His two full seasons with Jordan saw him prove to many that he had the racing acumen to match his obvious speed, and the way in which he gradually got the better of highly-rated team-mate Rubens Barrichello, was one of the reasons why he was able to clinch his shock move to Ferrari for 1996.

Life at Ferrari

To join any Formula One team as team-mate to Schumacher is not an enviable task, as it inevitably involves being shown up, made to look second best. Many drivers couldn't hack

IN THE POINTS: Eddie Irvine started his career at Ferrari with third place in Australia

such a comparison, but Eddie realised there was no disgrace in it, as everyone considers Schumacher to be the man of the moment in racing. He even thought he would learn a trick or two from the German to add to his own portfolio. He'd also be picking up a sizeable pay cheque and would be able to negotiate a good deal for spare parts for his own beloved road-going Ferrari 288 GTO…

However, some years Ferrari are up, and others they are not. Last season was generally down. The team had rediscovered its winning ways near the end of 1995, after a five-year drought, but there was still internal strife that only added to the problems when last year's car was not only very late in arriving, but proved not to be what it should have been. Panic set in and Schumacher was the one asked to sort it

out, leaving Eddie kicking his heels on the sidelines, denied the testing needed to really learn about the car.

The first race at Melbourne was a false dawn as both qualified well and Eddie finished third, albeit a country mile behind the two Williams drivers. He scored points in two of the next four Grands Prix, but then, with the team in increasing disarray, Eddie retired from the next nine races. Fortunately, he was able to end the year on an upbeat note, running more competitively in Italy, Portugal and Japan, albeit being hit by Berger in both of the last two.

For the season ahead, you can't help but feel that Ferrari will give Eddie a better and more reliable car, let him get some testing in before the season starts, and the results will surely flow.

TRACK NOTES

Nationality: ...... NORTHERN IRISH
Born: .... 10 NOVEMBER, 1965,
..... NEWTOWNARDS, N. IRELAND
Teams: .... JORDAN 1993–1995,
.... FERRARI 1996–1997

Career record

First Grand Prix start: ... 1993 JAPAN
Grand Prix starts: 50
Grand Prix wins: .... None
.. (best result: third, 1995 Canada;
.... 1996 Australia)
Poles: .... None
Fastest laps: .... None
Points: 28
Honours: 1993 JAPANESE FORMULA
3000 RUNNER-UP, 1987 BRITISH
FORMULA FORD CHAMPION &
FORMULA FORD FESTIVAL WINNER

HOTTEST DRIVE: Grand Prix debut at Suzuka when he qualified eighth, finished sixth and fought with Senna, literally…
BIGGEST SETBACK: Nine consecutive retirements for Ferrari in 1996.
MOST LIKELY TO SAY: "I haven't met a journalist who knows a thing about racing."
LEAST LIKELY TO SAY: "I was happy that Michael (Schumacher) got to do all the testing at Ferrari."

MORE, PLEASE!: Eddie Irvine collected just one trophy in 1996. Expect him to collect more this year

" Last year was the worst of my racing career.
EDDIE IRVINE **"**

OLIVIER PANIS

The glory of France

For any driver to win the Monaco Grand Prix it's special. For a Frenchman it's even more so. But for a Frenchman to score his maiden win there and to do it in a French car is the stuff that dreams are made of, just perfect to feature in a film script.

Yet, this is precisely what Olivier Panis managed to do in 1996, totally against the run of play, in one of the most peculiar Grands Prix of all time, at a circuit that has had more than its share of bizarre races. Yet no-one could say he was anything other than a deserving winner, for while those around him lost their heads, he kept his with devastating effect.

The day it all came right

That glorious day in Monaco last May the sun didn't shine. But it probably will be in Olivier's mind whenever he thinks back to it. In fact, the weather was truly terrible, with a race-morning deluge giving way to drizzle just before the race, leaving the track wet when the five red lights on the starting gantry flicked out to get the Grand Prix underway.

Sitting 14th on the grid, Olivier wasn't able to see that Damon Hill had got the jump on Michael Schumacher. He was also too busy getting himself placed for the first corner to notice why Jos Verstappen speared off there and too busy to look in his mirrors on the climb to Casino Square to see the Minardi twins Giancarlo Fisichella and Pedro Lamy crash behind him. He saw Schumacher later in the lap though, with his Ferrari mangled against the barriers before the tunnel, and Rubens Barrichello's Jordan likewise further on. He could have had no idea that the race would turn out so well for him.

Hill's engine failure when he was a runaway leader and Jean Alesi's retirement with broken suspension, after he had taken the lead, certainly helped him. But most of the credit must go to Olivier himself, for he was simply the one who read the conditions best and

picked his way diligently up the order, with only McLaren's David Coulthard close to him in the ever-changing conditions. It was, quite simply, the biggest upset in a decade, but Olivier never put a foot wrong and attacked while others were pussy-footing around. If he can produce a drive of anything close to that magnitude this year, he will give Ligier reason to smile again. But don't bet your last dollar on another win.

True blue Frenchman

France used to have a career path for its young drivers that was the envy of the world. Bankrolled primarily by Elf and Gitanes, it would gather the best of each age group and guide them from karts to Formula Renault, through Formula Three and into Formula 3000, with the very best being helped to make that final step into Formula One, preferably with France's main Grand Prix team: Ligier. But the machine has broken down, not helped by the passing of an act which outlawed cigarette and alcohol advertising in sporting circles, thus taking Gitanes out of the equation. And just last autumn, Elf said that it too was pulling out. The effect can already be seen as the cream of the current crop of French youngsters struggles to make the grade. Olivier was the last one to ride this conveyor belt to the top.

An ace in karting, Olivier won a Formula Renault scholarship in 1988 and was French champion the following year. He took two bites at the Formula Three cherry, being runner-up in the 1991 title race. Formula 3000 was yet another two-year project, and Olivier won the

GLORY RIDE: Olivier Panis's win in Monaco was the Ligier team's first for 15 years

TRACK NOTES

Nationality: . . . . FRENCH
Born: . . . . 2 SEPTEMBER, 1966,
. . . . LYON, FRANCE
Teams: . . . LIGIER/PROST 1994–1997

Career record

First Grand Prix start: . . 1994 BRAZIL
Grand Prix starts: 51
Grand Prix wins: 1
1996 . . . . *Monaco*
Poles: . . . . None
Fastest laps: . . . . None
Points: 44
Honours: . . . . 1993 FORMULA 3000
CHAMPION, 1991 FRENCH FORMULA
THREE RUNNER-UP, 1989 FRENCH
FORMULA RENAULT CHAMPION

HOTTEST DRIVE: Winning 1996
Monaco GP as others slid off
around him in the wet
BIGGEST SETBACK: Being outraced by
little-rated team-mate Pedro Diniz
in his home Grand Prix at Magny-
Cours in 1996
MOST LIKELY TO SAY: "France needs
its own Grand Prix team."
LEAST LIKELY TO SAY: "I would love to
drive for an English team."

HOW DID I DO THAT?: Olivier Panis ponders how he managed to win in Monaco, yet never mounted another rostrum in 1996

1993 Championship for the crack DAMS team. And there was the government-funded springboard to Formula One and a ride with Ligier. In his maiden Formula One season, Olivier astonished everyone by bringing his car home in all but one of the 16 Grands Prix. Impressive in any driver, it was doubly so in his rookie season, when a few "new-boy" mistakes are expected. He also scored more points than his more experienced team-mate Eric Bernard, and, not surprisingly, he kept the drive for 1995.

Improving on that 11th place overall in 1994, Olivier finished up eighth overall in 1995, helped largely by a surprise second place in the final race, in Australia, when he limped home with a smoking engine. Last season yielded ninth place overall, but all except three of his 13 points came from that glory day in Monaco, which says rather too much about the form of the Ligier team through the rest of the season. However, despite seven retirements, Olivier was always close to the points when he did finish, frustratingly finishing seventh (one place outside the points) on four occasions.

> **"** *I don't think I'll ever forget the sound of the yacht sirens in the harbour.*
> *OLIVIER PANIS* **"**

MIKA SALO

Waiting in the wings

Seen as one of Formula One's men of the future, Mika Salo is biding his time at Tyrrell until a top team picks him up and gives him a shot at Grand Prix glory.

Mika Salo and Mika Hakkinen share a Christian name, they share a nationality, and they both have typically Scandinavian fair hair and blue eyes. But ask either of them about their relationship and that's all they share. For these two Finns are not the best of friends, and it goes back a very long way.

Ask anyone else in Formula One what else this pair has in common, and they will tell you that both are blindingly fast, both capable of winning Grands Prix if armed with the right equipment. As yet, Hakkinen has come closer to their mutual goal with three second place

finishes to Salo's four fifths. But providing Salo keeps chipping away for Tyrrell through the season ahead and continues to impress the people who matter, then expect him to move to a loftier team for 1998, with a ride at Ferrari already being mentioned in despatches.

Finnish civil war

Following a year behind Hakkinen in the junior ranks, but going one better by winning the European Formula Ford crown ahead of Michael Schumacher, Salo caught up in 1989 when they both had troubled seasons in the

British Formula Three Championship. But, in 1990, they fought a fierce, season-long battle for glory in the same championship and, with three-quarters of the campaign over, Salo was ahead on points. But the balance tipped away from him when he spun out of the lead at one race and Hakkinen won both that particular race and the title. The separate paths of their subsequent racing careers is history.

Desired by many a team manager for their Formula 3000 programmes in 1991, yet without sufficient backing, Salo had to go to Japan to keep his momentum going. Yet all the top teams were full, and it took him several years before he was in a position to show his true ability.

Starting with a bang

To the people in Formula One though, Mika was forgotten, emphasising how little attention they pay to anyone outside their own world. His arrival in Formula One caused them to sit up and pay attention, as Mika did a more than competent job for the dying Lotus team at the end of 1994, never once spinning. Then he ran third in the first Grand Prix of 1995, in Brazil, before suffering cramp that forced him to drive largely one-handed. This eventually resulted in a spin and he dropped back to finish just out of the points in seventh place. All this in a Tyrrell, a car more usually found mid-order.

HOT PROPERTY: Many team managers will be watching Mika Salo very carefully in the season ahead

> *Going to Japan before Formula One made me much more patient.*
>
> MIKA SALO

THE OTHER MIKA: Mika Salo has always been out to beat compatriot Mika Hakkinen, even since their days in karts

TRACK NOTES

Nationality: . . . . FINNISH
Born: . . . . 30 NOVEMBER, 1966,
. . . . HELSINKI, FINLAND
Teams: . . . . LOTUS 1994,
. . . . TYRRELL 1995–1997

Career record
First Grand Prix start: . . . 1994 JAPAN
Grand Prix starts: 37
Grand Prix wins: . . . . None
*(best result: fifth, 1995 Italy,
Australia; 1996 Brazil, Monaco)*
Poles: . . . . None
Fastest laps: . . . . None
Points: 10
Honours: . . . 1990 BRITISH FORMULA
THREE RUNNER-UP, 1988 EUROPEAN
FORMULA FORD CHAMPION

HOTTEST DRIVE: Running third in 1995
Brazilian GP before suffering cramp,
spinning and falling back to seventh
BIGGEST SETBACK: Losing backing to
graduate to Formula 3000 in 1991,
sending him to Japan, then taking
several years to land a
competitive drive
MOST LIKELY TO SAY: "Give me a top
car and I will win races."
LEAST LIKELY TO SAY: "Mika Hakkinen
is the best Finnish driver."

Despite this impressive start with Tyrrell, Mika started making mistakes as he fought to secure points and scored on only three occasions in 1995, with two of these scores coming in the last two Grands Prix. The Tyrrell chassis was clearly not one of the team's best – experienced team-mate Uyko Katayama failed to score even once – so it was clear who was going to be the team's number one driver when they both stayed on for last season, even though it was through the Japanese driver that the team got its works Yamaha engines.

Last year, the Tyrrell chassis was considerably better, but Formula One fans became accustomed to seeing the underfunded cars from Surrey pull off with far, far too many engine failures, giving the drivers little chance to shine or score points.

Ken Tyrrell has seen drivers come and go over the three decades he has been running a team since he started with Jackie Stewart as lead driver in the 1960s. So he knows a good driver when he sees one, and is why he fought tooth and nail last autumn to retain Salo's services for 1997, with the new Stewart Grand Prix team chief among those looking to steal him away. While Tyrrell lost out to Arrows in the battle to hang on to Yamaha engines, he kept hold of his spiky-haired, roller-blading driver. For this year, at least.

MICHAEL SCHUMACHER

Million Dollar Man

He's worth a second a lap they say, in whatever he drives. No wonder Michael Schumacher is a double World Champion and is paid a million dollars per race by Ferrari.

Michael Schumacher is the best racing driver in the world. Do not discuss, it's a fact. Since Ayrton Senna died in 1994, the German has assumed this mantle. Indeed, in the two races Senna contested that year, he was beaten both times by Schumacher, so perhaps he was about to have to hand over the crown anyway.

No driver likes to admit that another driver is faster, for it hurts not only their ego but also their future earning potential. However, there is not a driver in Formula One who can claim to be faster than Michael. He's got two World Championships to his name, whereas arguably lesser talents from the past such as Nelson Piquet managed to score three. But that's just for starters, as Michael is sure to collect many more.

Just as he will continue to dazzle and out-perform those around him, even when he's at the wheel of noticeably inferior equipment, such as last year's Ferrari.

It was once said that Michael was worth a second a lap in whatever car he drove. This may be slightly generous, but it's a figure few can quibble with. And this is precisely why Ferrari raided the bank to employ him for 1996 and beyond. And their reward was rich. Driving a car that was not good enough to win races, he did so on three occasions and has given the team a focus as it heads into the new season,

> **" Ferrari can do it.**
> Michael Schumacher **"**

the one in which Michael predicted he would be going not just for race wins, but for the world title.

Talent-spotted

Michael was a top-notch kart racer in his youth. But you'd expect this of anyone whose father owned a kart circuit. However, the skill was there for all to see, especially when he burst into car racing in 1988 and was spotted by Willi Weber, a man with wealth from the film industry. He took control of Michael's career, guiding him through Formula Three, in which he showed a flash of the brilliance that was to follow by winning one of the heats of the Macau Formula Three Grand Prix in 1989. A year later, with the German Formula Three crown in his pocket, he won at Macau, albeit only after pressuring Mika Hakkinen into making a mistake. By this time, he was also a race-winning works sportscar driver for Mercedes.

Continuing with sportscars in 1991, while he tried to land a drive in Formula

MICHAEL'S DAY OF DAYS: Winning in Spain was almost a miracle, but winning in front of the *tifosi* at Monza was the ultimate

3000, Michael was offered the chance to make his Formula One debut, for Jordan at the Belgian Grand Prix. This opportunity had arisen as regular driver Bertrand Gachot had been sent to prison for squirting CS gas in the face of a London taxi driver. Michael made the most of it, qualifying seventh, four places ahead of the team's other driver, Andrea de Cesaris. He was then poached by Benetton in a straight swap for its second driver, Roberto Moreno. The points started flowing straight away. He even out-qualified team-mate Piquet in four of the five remaining races.

Life at Benetton

Over the next four seasons with Benetton, Michael scored his first win in Belgium in 1992, en route to third place in the championship. Another victory followed in 1993, but in 1994 it all came right, when Michael won eight races despite being prevented from starting on two occasions as a result of an unsuccessful appeal against his exclusion from the British Grand Prix. It all came to a head at the final race in Australia, when he clipped the wall when leading and appeared to drive into title rival Damon Hill at the next corner, and took both of them out. In so doing, he claimed the World Championship. No-one thought he didn't deserve it, but few respected the way he clinched it.

His second World Championship was claimed in a far more acceptable manner as he took the battle to Hill's superior Williams, and yet came out with nine wins to the Englishman's four, meaning that the title was his with two races still to run.

Then, racing for Ferrari last year, Michael had an even steeper mountain to climb. He had moved to a team that knew little about winning on a regular basis, save for those team members with very long memories.

TRACK NOTES

Nationality:	.... GERMAN
Born:	.... 3 JANUARY, 1969,
	.... KERPEN, GERMANY
Teams:	.... JORDAN 1991,
	.... BENETTON 1991–1995,
	.... FERRARI 1996–1997

Career record

First Grand Prix start:	1991 BELGIUM
Grand Prix starts:	 87
Grand Prix wins:	 22
1992	.... Belgium
1993	.... Portugal
1994	.. Brazil, Pacific, San Marino, Monaco, Canada, France, Hungary, Europe
1995	.... Brazil, Spain, Monaco, France, Germany, Belgium, Europe, Pacific, Japan
1996	.... Spain, Belgium, Italy
Poles:	 14
Fastest laps:	 25
Points:	 368
Honours:	.... 1995 & 1994 FORMULA ONE WORLD CHAMPION, 1990 GERMAN FORMULA THREE CHAMPION & MACAU GP WINNER, 1988 GERMAN FORMULA KONIG CHAMPION

HOTTEST DRIVE: Trouncing the opposition in wet 1996 Spanish GP
BIGGEST SETBACK: None
MOST LIKELY TO SAY: "Eddie (Irvine) is the best team-mate I've ever had."
LEAST LIKELY TO SAY: "I really hope I can keep up with Damon."

NOTHING BUT THE BEST WILL DO:
Michael Schumacher's disappointment was obvious after he qualified behind both Williams at Spa

JACQUES VILLENEUVE

The smart-cookie rookie

He came, he saw and he damn near conquered in his very first year of Formula One. Jacques Villeneuve starts 1997 as the championship favourite for Williams.

To think that Jacques Villeneuve was able to take the battle of the second generation drivers down to the final round of last year's Formula One World Championship is incredible, a testament to his speed and his ability to learn.

Sure, he famously fluffed his start that day at Suzuka and fell from pole to sixth by the first corner, then a wheel fell off and instantly turned his Williams team-mate Damon Hill into the World Champion, but it was only his first season in Formula One against Hill's fifth. In that time he had not only learned the car and the tracks, but he had got the team behind him, rather than behind Hill. It was extraordinary, but Jacques is very much a smart cookie for a rookie.

His late father Gilles was also a past master at getting a team behind him. But that was achieved in a totally different way for, while Gilles earned their undying devotion through his naïvety, Jacques is far more calculated, well versed in the psychological war that's all the rage in all top sports these days. Much as he will try to deny it, the evidence of this scheming is there for all to see.

Not at all like his father

However, the fact that he is being kept on by Williams for 1997 and Hill is not, is down not only to shrewd contract negotiations by his manager Craig Pollock, but also to the way that he knuckled down and learned his craft in Formula One, indeed out-performing Hill in the second half of last season. Where father Gilles was fast and flamboyant, sideways everywhere, that is not Jacques's chosen style. He's fast and smooth instead. But then he's Jacques, not Gilles, as he often tells people when they try to see him as a clone of his father.

Always his own man, Jacques was never that enamoured with racing as a child, when he, his mother and his sister trailed around after Gilles. However, Jacques found himself giving racing a shot when he left school and he was caught up in it all, racing for three seasons in the Italian Formula Three Championship with increasing speed, but no wins and no sign of his latent promise. Moving to the Japanese Formula Three series in 1992, he started winning and ended the season as runner-up. This gave him the

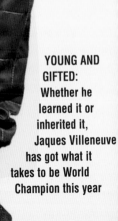

YOUNG AND GIFTED: Whether he learned it or inherited it, Jaques Villeneuve has got what it takes to be World Champion this year

COOL CUSTOMER: Villeneuve swiftly mastered every move in his rise to becoming a major player, using team politics as well as computer track simulations to his advantage

> ## " *Hill and I both made mistakes, but he did a better season than I did.* "
> ### JACQUES VILLENEUVE

confidence to go and race in the North American Formula Atlantic Championship the following year, where Jacques placed third overall, and was adjudged top rookie.

For 1994, he made the step up to Indycars, was sixth overall and again was selected as best rookie in North America's top formula. He also finished second in the Indianapolis 500, America's biggest race, much to the chagrin of the regulars. Then, brushing aside far more experienced rivals, Jacques won the Indianapolis 500 in 1995, and recorded three other victories to walk off with the Indycar title.

So, the speed and racecraft that Jacques brought with him to Formula One was clearly no fluke. After all, Indycars travel at speeds of up to 240mph. What Jacques had to concentrate on more was learning the technicalities of the Formula One car which are very different to the heavier, more powerful and less technically advanced Indycars; rather like a race horse next to a cart horse.

Learning the circuits

Top drivers will tell you that if you're good, you will learn a circuit that's new to you in just four or five laps. So, maybe Jacques wasn't at such a large disadvantage as people made out when he turned up to race on a circuit that was new to him in 1996. Indeed, when he went to Spa-Francorchamps for the Belgian Grand Prix, he qualified on pole, and put much of the credit for this down to learning the "flow" of the circuit by playing a Formula One computer simulation game. A child of the times, indeed.

What should become even more apparent is how Jacques has continued to gel with the Williams team personnel, especially with joint team principal Patrick Head, how his ever increasing knowledge of the car and its technology, the tracks and the way the team works has boosted his confidence. He could perform on an even higher plane than 1996, which will give highly-rated new team-mate Heinz-Harald Frentzen food for thought.

TRACK NOTES

Nationality: . . . . CANADIAN
Born: . . . . 9 APRIL, 1971,
 ST JEAN-SUR-RICHELIEU, CANADA
Teams: . . . . . . WILLIAMS 1996–1997

Career record
First Grand Prix start: 1996 AUSTRALIA
Grand Prix starts: 18
Grand Prix wins: 5
 1996 . Europe, Britain, Hungary,
 Portugal
 1997 . . . . Brazil
Poles: 5
Fastest laps: 7
Points: 88
Honours: . . . . 1996 FORMULA ONE
 RUNNER-UP, 1995 INDYCAR
CHAMPION, 1994 INDYCAR ROOKIE OF
 THE YEAR, 1993 TOYOTA ATLANTIC
ROOKIE OF THE YEAR, 1992 JAPANESE
 FORMULA THREE RUNNER-UP

HOTTEST DRIVE: Winning the 1995
 Indianapolis 500
BIGGEST SETBACK: Falling back to
 sixth at Suzuka in the last race of
 1996, having started on pole
MOST LIKELY TO SAY: "Just wait until
 1997."
LEAST LIKELY TO SAY: "That's enough
 of me, let's talk about my father's
 racing career."

RUBENS BARRICHELLO

Young at heart

Weaned on karts and single-seaters, Rubens Barrichello was the boy wonder who would follow Ayrton Senna. But his star already needs to brighten again — and he's not yet 25.

REFRESHING CHANGE: Barrichello is looking forward to a new start with Stewart

It was handed on a plate to Rubens Barrichello. Unbelievably talented in karts, he scared his rivals into keeping a jump ahead of him rather than come face to face. People took notice wherever he went. And a consortium of Brazilian businessmen took the unprecedented step after Rubens had done just one year in Formula Ford of offering him a deal that would take him to Europe, all expenses paid, and hopefully all the way to Formula One. Then, and only then, would they want anything in return. The ultimate ticket to ride!

Thus freed from financial worries, Rubens was left to what he does best: racing. Two titles in two years in Europe, first the European Formula Opel series in 1990 and then British Formula Three Championship set people thinking the second Messiah had come.

Rubens even drove for the same team, West Surrey Racing, with whom compatriot and hero Ayrton Senna had won the British Formula Three title some eight years before.

After a mixed season in Formula 3000 in 1992, Formula One was waiting and in Jordan, Rubens found a team that would offer him a family atmosphere, make the Grand Prix world less daunting for a 20-year-old who was, in many ways, years younger than that except when behind the wheel. It mattered little to them that away from the track his was a world of computer games and other juvenile pastimes when he could put in drives like the one that saw him run second to Senna in the wet at Donington Park, in only his third Grand Prix.

That was the beginning, but this is now. The golden boy has lost his sheen after four largely fruitless years at Jordan. Sure, he's been on the podium twice in a car that was not capable of challenging for victory, but the big teams such as McLaren and Ferrari are no longer seeking his services. At the end of 1996, even Jordan didn't want to keep him and he considered racing Indycars.

A new beginning

However, for 1997, Rubens has joined the new Stewart Grand Prix team, and it's wake-up time. Time for someone to reawaken a wonderfully natural skill, re-light the fire that burned before Senna died. Many believe Rubens has never been the same since that weekend in May 1994. True, he cheated death himself in a huge shunt two days beforehand, but it's more the expectations of Brazil having fallen on his young shoulders that has troubled him, and that he gave up on last year's Jordan, considering it uncompetitive. Rubens doesn't need a driving coach, he needs someone to

TRACK NOTES

Nationality: .... BRAZILIAN
Born: .... 23 MAY, 1972,
.... SAO PAULO, BRAZIL
Teams: ...... JORDAN 1993–1996,
.... STEWART 1997

Career record

First Grand Prix start: ....
.... .1993 SOUTH AFRICAN GP
Grand Prix starts: 66
Grand Prix wins: .... None
(best result: second, 1995 Canadian GP)
Poles: 1
Fastest laps: .... None
Points: 46
Honours: . . 1991 BRITISH FORMULA THREE CHAMPION,
1990 GM EUROSERIES CHAMPION,
1988 BRAZILIAN KARTING CHAMPION

HOTTEST DRIVE: Running second to Ayrton Senna in wet 1993 European GP at Donington Park
BIGGEST SETBACK: Retiring six laps from end of that same race
MOST LIKELY TO SAY: "Jackie Stewart is so professional."
LEAST LIKELY TO SAY: "I wish I could return to Jordan."

help him grow up and to give him adult confidence. Then, and only then, will he dazzle again. Joining Stewart Grand Prix could be just the move he's been waiting for.

PEDRO DINIZ

Poor little rich kid

Pedro Diniz is very, very rich. He is also a Formula One driver and he is determined to prove in his third season that he deserves to be the latter even without his family money.

Being as rich as Croesus is all well and good, and it can certainly open all the doors on your route to Formula One. Indeed, it has done just this for Pedro Diniz. But it can also mask your skill behind the wheel as people only see the size of your wallet, not the extent of your ability.

When the sport's insiders are asked what they think of Olivier Panis's driving skills, they will say that he is a highly competent individual, held back primarily by the French Ligier he drives not being a top-line car. His win in last year's Monaco Grand Prix was a just reward for his diligence. And Pedro? Oh, he's only in Formula One because of his money. And do you remember how slow he was in that Forti in 1995, dreadful, but always on the television screens as he was lapped time and again by the front runners. But this is not fair; it is a case of people seeing what they want to see.

Better than people think

For example, Diniz out-qualified team-mate Panis for the French Grand Prix last year and ran ahead of him for fully 28 laps until retiring. This on a track which Panis almost grew up on. Even team-mate Roberto Moreno, who is certainly no slouch, struggled in the awfully underdeveloped Forti two seasons ago. So, maybe Pedro is not as bad as people think, and it's clear to those who choose to look that he's making progress all the time, much as his 1997 team-mate Damon Hill did in his career.

Unlike so many of his contemporaries though, Pedro only had a brief shot at racing karts. Encouraged by his father who was a racer in his youth, he did a season of Formula Ford in Brazil that was followed in 1990 by a season in the South American Formula Three Championship, before heading to the British series in 1991, in which he drove for West Surrey Racing alongside compatriot Rubens Barrichello. This produced just one points-scoring

TRACK NOTES

Nationality: . . . . BRAZILIAN
Born: . . . . 22 MAY, 1970,
. . . . SAO PAULO, BRAZIL
Teams: . . . . . . FORTI CORSE 1995,
. . . . . LIGIER 1996, ARROWS 1997

Career record

First Grand Prix start: . . . .
. . . . 1995 BRAZILIAN GP
Grand Prix starts: 35
Grand Prix wins: . . . . None
(best result: sixth, 1996 Spanish
GP & 1996 Italian GP)
Poles: . . . . None
Fastest laps: . . . . None
Points: 2
Honours: . . . . None

HOTTEST DRIVE: 1996 French GP when he led team-mate Olivier Panis for much of race
BIGGEST SETBACK: Spending first year in Formula One with Forti
MOST LIKELY TO SAY: "I'm not only in Formula One because of my money."
LEAST LIKELY TO SAY: "Can anyone lend me five quid."

THIRD TIME LUCKY?
Pedro Diniz is hoping that his move to Arrows will establish him

drive, but things went better when he moved to Edenbridge Racing in 1992 and collected a pair of third places.

Formula 3000 came next and he spent two seasons with Forti Corse, showing flashes of speed but general inconsistency, peaking with fourth place at Estoril in 1994 before graduating with them to Formula One in 1995. Looking back, he probably wishes he had taken his money elsewhere...

That Pedro's first point came in last year's Spanish Grand Prix is proof that many of the front runners fell off. But, hand it to him, Pedro survived the torrential conditions. He also repeated the feat at Monza. So, for 1997, expect more points and more progress from one of the most pleasant men in Formula One.

GIANCARLO FISICHELLA

Italy's great new hope

Italian fans have little to cheer about these days, with Giovanni Lavaggi their only representative in some races in 1996. So they will welcome Fisichella back with open arms.

TRACK NOTES

Nationality: . . . . ITALIAN
Born: . . . . 14 JANUARY, 1973,
. . . . ROME, ITALY
Teams: . . . . MINARDI 1996,
. . . . JORDAN 1997

Career record
First Grand Prix start: . . . .
. . . . 1996 AUSTRALIAN GP
Grand Prix starts: 10
Grand Prix wins: . . . . None
(best result: eighth 1996 Canadian GP, 1997 Brazilian GP)
Poles: . . . . None
Fastest laps: . . . . None
Points: . . . . None
Honours: 1994 ITALIAN FORMULA THREE CHAMPION, 1991 EUROPEAN KART RUNNER-UP

HOTTEST DRIVE: Winning the 1994 Monaco Formula Three Grand Prix
BIGGEST SETBACK: Being dropped by Minardi to make way for Giovanni Lavaggi
MOST LIKELY TO SAY: "We need more power."
LEAST LIKELY TO SAY: "I never want to drive for Ferrari."

There's something very exciting about Giancarlo Fisichella. He is cut from the right cloth to be the perfect Italian racing driver: small, dark, with a cheeky face, great speed in the car and a temperament to match. He was even spotted crying for joy on a podium after a touring car race last year. Yes, he is someone the _tifosi_ could take to their hearts, someone to guide them into the next millennium. And if he were to do so in a race-winning Ferrari, their joy would know no bounds.

However, he has first to put a full season behind him. Last year's foray into Grand Prix racing was only a partial one as financial considerations meant that the Minardi team could only afford to field him until the British Grand Prix after which he was stood down in favour his less able compatriot Lavaggi. In fact, his lack of budget had already seen him miss the two South American races because Tarso Marques brought the team much needed cash.

Giancarlo was a karting legend in Italy, before challenging for the European crown over the next few seasons. A year in Formula Alfa Boxer was followed by three seasons in the Italian Formula Three Championship. Runner-up in the second year, he followed this up by winning the title in 1994, when he also won the Monaco Formula Three Grand Prix and one of the two heats in Macau.

Saved by touring cars

Then came the standard problem of not having enough money to progress to Formula 3000. Fortunately for Giancarlo, Alfa Romeo was looking for young talent to feed into its International Touring Car Championship team. Mercedes wanted him too, but Alfa won the

TWO-WAY STRETCH: Giancarlo Fisichella raced for Minardi and Alfa Romeo in 1996

battle and Giancarlo has spent the past two years in this high-tech arena. He made an instant impact by finishing second in only his second race. Results in his second season were better still. But ever since his first run as Minardi's test driver in 1995, Giancarlo has had only one career direction: to Formula One.

In the eight Grands Prix Giancarlo contested last year, his highest finish was eighth, in the Canadian Grand Prix. But there were dark days, too; in Monaco he collided with team-mate Pedro Lamy on the opening lap, taking both out. And in Spain at the very next race when the same pair pulled off the same trick, again on the opening lap.

However, his second season in Formula One will see him having a full campaign, this time with Jordan. He pipped Martin Brundle for the second seat, convincing the team that youthful speed rather than guile and experience was the way to go. Take note, though, that Benetton's Flavio Briatore is very keen to secure his services for 1998.

UKYO KATAYAMA

The man from Japan

Having shone as Japan's big hope in 1994, it's been a thin time for this likeable lightweight ever since. But he's not given up trying and is going to be giving his all for Minardi.

Feted in Japan as the best home-grown talent in Formula 3000 in the early 1990s, Ukyo made his Formula One debut with the Venturi Larrousse team in 1992. However, it will be a shock to see him race for Minardi this year as it's with Tyrrell that Ukyo will always be associated. Like the scarcely liveried flanks of the underfinanced cars, Ukyo's blue, red and white helmet seemed part of the fixtures and fittings as it poked out of the cockpit. Or, at the start of the 1996 season, didn't poke out of the cockpit. Ukyo is short, very short. And the new car sported the regulation higher cockpit sides for greater driver protection, ergo a lack of view for our little hero. Changes, as you can imagine, had to be made so that he could see what he was doing.

Ukyo's aerobatic display

That it got to this late stage before discovering this drawback was largely to do with Ukyo having spent the winter of 1995–96 recovering from a wildly spectacular accident he endured at the start of the 1995 Portuguese Grand Prix. This, ladies and gentlemen, was no ordinary shunt, but an aerial twister as the cars left the grid that saw Ukyo vault over several other cars before striking the pit wall. Silence fell as the dust and debris settled and, amazingly, out

stepped Ukyo. No bones were broken, but the shaking left him with headaches for months and in no fit state to do any physical training.

If in 1995 the Tyrrell chassis was not what it had been when Ukyo had often appeared in the top placings in the 1994 season before inevitably retiring, last year the problem was with the team's Yamaha engines going pop with annoying regularity. It was this lack of results – seventh place was his highest finish in a pointless season – that led to people suggesting that it was time that Ukyo stood

down from Formula One and let younger compatriots have a go. However, Ukyo was not ready to go. And if you doubt his commitment, don't forget that Ukyo took the unusual step of racing in France early in his career as well as assorted outings in the unloved Footwork chassis in European Formula 3000, before going back to Japan to win the 1991 Japanese Formula 3000 title and raise the finance to graduate to Formula One. He is a very determined individual, and desperate for one last shot before he heads home.

TRACK NOTES

Nationality: . . . . JAPANESE
Born: . . . . 29 MAY, 1963,
. . . . TOKYO, JAPAN
Teams: . VENTURI LARROUSSE 1992,
TYRRELL 1993–96, MINARDI 1997

Career record

First Grand Prix start: . . . .
. . . . . . 1992 SOUTH AFRICAN GP
Grand Prix starts: 80
Grand Prix wins: . . . . None
(best result: fifth, 1994 Brazilian GP
& 1994 San Marino GP)
Poles: . . . . None
Fastest laps: . . . . None
Points: 5
Honours: 1991 JAPANESE FORMULA
3000 CHAMPION, 1984 JAPANESE
FJ1600 CHAMPION

HOTTEST DRIVE: Running fourth in
1994 Italian GP before retiring
BIGGEST SETBACK: Flipping at start of
1995 Portuguese GP at Estoril.
MOST LIKELY TO SAY: "I made a
stupid mistake."
LEAST LIKELY TO SAY: "The engine
never lets me down."

LAST SHOT: Ukyo Katayama is back for one last crack at Formula One

NICOLA LARINI

Back where he belongs

Formula One has never been kind to Larini, and years with the wrong teams saw him quit for touring cars. Bouncing back with a Ferrari-powered Sauber is his biggest chance yet.

This little Italian could be one of Formula One's older statesmen by now as he not only started in the sport's top category as long ago as 1987, but he went on to become a Ferrari driver. However, it was not to be. Yet a surprise move last winter that saw the Sauber team land a deal to use Ferrari engines meant that he was back, for he was part of the deal.

And no-one can begrudge Larini his return alongside Johnny Herbert. After an exemplary career in the junior ranks, during which he won the Italian Formula Three title in 1986, he was in Formula One by the end of 1987. Trouble was, this promotion was with the little-fancied Coloni team. And 1988 was little better as he had to face up to the uphill struggle of qualifying the Alfa-powered Osella. And his reward for making the cut more often than not? A ride with Osella in 1989 when he generally failed to advance further than the pre-qualifying season that eliminated the slowest cars before qualifying proper began. However, late in the season, Larini made marked progress and attracted the attention of the Ligier team for 1990.

This was Larini's chance to impress in a midfield car rather than a tail-ender. But it yielded no points, with Larini twice just one place out of the points. So, it was time to pack up and move again, to the Lamborghini-powered Modena team for 1991. Seventh place first time out at Phoenix was a false dawn, for he finished three laps down. And the rest of the year was a disaster.

A Ferrari man

All was not lost, though, for he picked up a testing contract with Ferrari and finally got to drive a competitive Formula One car, just as he dropped down from Formula One to race touring cars. And here Larini really made his

FERRARI TESTER: But Nicola Larini will only have a Ferrari engine in 1997

mark, winning the Italian title for Alfa Romeo in 1992, then the German title for the Italian marque the following year. And each year since has seen him at the front, but all the while pining to return to Formula One.

During this spell, Larini was given four Grand Prix outings by Ferrari, two in 1992 when he replaced Ivan Capelli, then two more when standing in for the injured Jean Alesi in 1994, claiming second place in the San Marino GP behind Schumacher's Benetton on that dark day when Ayrton Senna died.

There was a great deal of pressure for Larini to be promoted from Ferrari's test team to be Michael Schumacher's number two in 1996, but Eddie Irvine got the nod. And then, with the International Touring Car Championship in which he raced crumbling at the end of last season, the timing was just right for him to leap in with Sauber.

TRACK NOTES

Nationality: . . . . ITALIAN
Born: . . . . 19 MARCH, 1964,
. . . . . . LIDO DI CAMAIORE. ITALY
Teams: . . . . COLONI 1987,
. OSELLA 1988-1989, LIGIER 1990,
MODENA 1991, FERRARI 1992 AND
. . . . 1994, SAUBER 1997

Career record

First Grand Prix start: . . . .
. . . . 1987 SPANISH GP
Grand Prix starts: 47
. . . . . . (best result: second, 1994
. . . . San Marino GP)
Grand Prix wins: . . . . None
Poles: . . . . None
Fastest laps: . . . . None
Points: 6
Honours: . . . 1993 GERMAN TOURING
CAR CHAMPION, 1992 ITALIAN
TOURING CAR CHAMPION, 1986
ITALIAN FORMULA THREE CHAMPION

HOTTEST DRIVE: To second place at
Imola in 1994
BIGGEST SETBACK: Not keeping Ferrari
drive at end of 1992
MOST LIKELY TO SAY: "Ferrari drivers
should be Italian."
LEAST LIKELY TO SAY: "You should
only have one shot at Formula One."

JARNO TRULLI

A man in a hurry

No one has ever reached Formula One as fast as Jarno Trulli. Not even idol Ayrton Senna. Just two years ago the Italian was racing karts, but now he's in Formula One with Minardi.

People may decry the occasional performance of some of Formula One's tail-enders, but no fool makes it to racing's big time without an extraordinary amount of driving ability. Apart from exceptional talents such as Michael Schumacher, the majority are separated by the equipment with which they are armed. So it's always exciting to true fans when an exciting young racer arrives on the Grand Prix scene, for each of these may turn out to be the next superstar.

Jarno Trulli is one such driver. And his ascent from the little-exposed world of karting to Formula One has been so rapid that many in the sport failed even to notice his approach. You can be sure, though, that they will soon be fully aware of this 22-year-old's skills as he explores the limits in his Minardi.

Friends in high places

Chief among those who have helped him rise from karting to Formula One in just two seasons is none other than Benetton team owner Flavio Briatore. Perhaps anxious to find himself a replacement for

QUICK LEARNER: Jarno Trulli's rise to F1 was fast

former charge Schumacher, Briatore financed Trulli's graduation through Formula Three. After a hugely successful career in karts that yielded World and Italian titles aplenty, Briatore paid for Trulli to jump direct to the German Formula Three series in a car liveried to look like a smaller version of a Benetton.

Starting halfway through the 1995 campaign, on tracks unfamiliar to him, Trulli won the final two races of the season and carried on in this vein at the start of 1996, again with the KMS team. Despite clearly not having the best car or the best engine, Trulli was still champion with races in hand. Talk of a run in Formula 3000 in 1997 held no interest to Trulli. Formula One would suit him instead, he said. Nice idea, people thought. But then, as the racers were almost under orders for the

TRACK NOTES

Nationality:	ITALIAN
Born:	13 JULY, 1974, PESCARA, ITALY
Teams:	MINARDI 1997

Career record

First Grand Prix start:	1997 AUSTRALIAN GP
Grand Prix starts:	2
Grand Prix wins:	None
	(best result: ninth, 1997 AUSTRALIAN GP)
Poles:	None
Fastest laps:	None
Points:	None
Honours:	1996 GERMAN FORMULA THREE CHAMPION, 1994 WORLD KARTING CHAMPION

HOTTEST DRIVE: Winning opening two rounds of 1996 German Formula Three series
BIGGEST SETBACK: None, as yet.
MOST LIKELY TO SAY: "People expect too much of me."
LEAST LIKELY TO SAY: "I wish I'd done Formula 3000."

first race, Briatore gave Trulli the nod and put him into the Minardi line-up in place of Tarso Marques. Briatore is a major share-holder in Minardi, you see. Now it's up to this precocious youth. And those who know him are sure that this will prove the dawning of a new talent on the world stage. Trulli will probably never win races in a Minardi, but he looks sure to put it far higher up the grid than it deserves to be. Certainly, he is expected to outpace team-mate Ukyo Katayama before long, especially when he has got a few races under his belt and gains confidence.

People have likened him to Senna, and he even bears a striking physical resemblance to the great man.

JAN MAGNUSSEN

The next Senna?

With a talent not seen since the late Ayrton Senna dominated Formula Three, Jan Magnussen could stun in Formula One, as long as he's kept under control by Stewart Grand Prix.

Not every year does a driver turn up in Formula One who looks capable of making people sit up and pay attention. But Jan Magnussen has the skills to do just that. Whether he impresses people from the front, middle or the rear of the grid depends on how quick the new Stewart Grand Prix team's challenger turns out to be.

They say Jan has talent to burn. After all, his 14 wins from 18 races in the 1994 British Formula Three Championship beat the previous record established by the late great Ayrton Senna in the days when the championship was not as competitive. However, Jan had been able to race in Formula Three only because Jackie Stewart had spotted his talent when he raced in Formula Ford (winning the Formula Ford Festival), and in Formula Opel when he was a front-runner in an underfinanced car and agreed to run him in his son Paul's team at a very special rate.

Despite his outstanding success with Paul Stewart Racing, Jan had no money to graduate to

RUDDY CHEEKS: Jan may look baby-faced but he drives like a veteran

Formula 3000, and coming from a country with as little industry as Denmark, had little hope of attracting any. So, with his single-seater career at the crossroads, Jan opted for a fully paid works ride with Mercedes in the International Touring Car Championship for which he would at least be paid.

Other drivers who accepted this lifeline crowed about how it was a more meaningful route to Formula One than via Formula 3000, the ITC cars running with an amazing array of technology including traction control and anti-lock brakes. But Jan wasn't among them and, although a front-runner, he couldn't wait to return to single-seaters and leapt at a chance to race in the 1995 Pacific Grand Prix for McLaren, for whom he was test driver, when Mika Hakkinen had appendicitis. Jan made the most of this opportunity, finishing in 10th place just behind team-mate Mark Blundell after a great scrap with Rubens Barrichello's Jordan.

Impressed by the USA

Then, last year, he tried his hand at Indycars in addition to his ITC programme, turning out for the Mercedes-powered Penske team in the final four races, thanks to Mercedes realising that single-seaters were his strongest suit. Impressing all who watched him, he occasionally out-paced his very experienced team-mates Al Unser Jr and Paul Tracy. And he loved the relaxed atmosphere, feeling this would suit a man of his laid-back nature far better than the uptight world of Formula One. But, after intense persuasion by Jackie Stewart, Jan agreed to stop eating junk food, give up smoking, take up fitness training and give Formula One a go. No doubt his manager was delighted with the four-year contract offered by Stewart Grand Prix...

As out-and-out racers go, Jan is one of the best, and to cap this, he's also thoroughly entertaining company with a strong sense of humour. Whether Stewart Grand Prix can turn him into a smartly turned-out corporate man remains to be seen.

TRACK NOTES

Nationality: . . . . DANISH
Born: . . . . 4 JULY, 1973,
. . . . ROSKILDE, DENMARK
Teams: . . . . McCLAREN 1995,
. . . . STEWART 1997

Career record

First Grand Prix start: 1995 PACIFIC GP
Grand Prix starts: 3
Grand Prix wins: . . . . None
(best result: 10th, 1995 Pacific GP)
Poles: . . . . None
Fastest laps: . . . . None
Points: . . . . None
Honours: . . 1994 BRITISH FORMULA THREE CHAMPION, 1992 FORMULA FORD FESTIVAL WINNER

HOTTEST DRIVE: Finishing 10th in 1995 Pacific GP
BIGGEST SETBACK: Never having any money
MOST LIKELY TO SAY: "Do I have to wear a jacket and tie...."
LEAST LIKELY TO SAY: "I love racing touring cars."

SHINJI NAKANO

Eastern promise

Ukyo Katayama came to Formula One and promised to give Japanese drivers a good name. But he failed and now it's Shinji Nakano's turn, starting this year with Ligier.

Shinji Nakano is the driver who could be the biggest surprise of 1997. Not because he is likely to suddenly start winning races for Ligier, but because he is virtually unknown to racing fans in Europe.

Shinji had been pencilled in as one of the drivers for the Japanese Dome team's foray into Formula One, but it was decided to delay this until the 1998 season, and so mid-season last year he started to be mooted as a candidate for the second Ligier seat alongside Olivier Panis for 1997.

However, no-one thought he had much of a chance thanks to a long line of France's finest young drivers also being in the reckoning, which would fit in well with pressure for Ligier to become an all-French outfit again. However, Shinji has friends in high places, such as at Mugen, Ligier's engine suppliers, and an impressive test with the French team at the end of last October put him to the head of the queue.

That he followed this up with two more strong tests, in which he not only set some flying times, but also showed good technical understanding and strong feed-back to the engineers, impressed further. And so he landed the drive, cutting across the bows of the French hopefuls. It's worth mentioning that Benetton boss Flavio Briatore owns Ligier too, and wanted to keep in the good books of the Japanese engine supplier. Benetton is faced with finding new engines for 1998 as current engine supplier Renault has made it clear that this is its last year in Formula One.

Watched over by Nakajima

Once a protégé of Japan's leading former Grand Prix racer Satoru Nakajima – a team-mate of Ayrton Senna's at Lotus in 1987 – he raced briefly in Europe in early 1990s, but that was in the junior formulae and thus out of the gaze of most Formula One fans. After a starring role in Japanese karting circles, in which he landed two national titles, Shinji had a year in Japanese Formula Three before contesting the British Formula Vauxhall Championship in 1990. He raced in the Euroseries for Paul Stewart Racing in 1991 and has thus tried many of the circuits on which he will be racing this year. But, he then headed back home to Japan where he moved directly to Formula 3000, albeit with little success in 1992.

Shinji stepped back down to Formula Three and found his form again in 1993, finishing fifth in a year when Tom Kristensen swept all before him. Three more seasons of Formula 3000 followed, with Shinji peaking with strong form in the unusual Dome chassis in 1996, claiming two second places en route to being classified sixth overall. This year he will be reunited with 1996 rival Ralf Schumacher.

TRACK NOTES

Nationality: . . . . JAPANESE
Born: . 1 APRIL, 1971, OSAKA, JAPAN
Teams: . . . . PROST 1997

Career record
First Grand Prix start: . . . .
. . . . .1997 AUSTRALIAN GP
Grand Prix starts: 2
Grand Prix wins: None *(best finish: seventh, 1997 Australian GP)*
Poles: . . . . None
Fastest laps: . . . . None
Points: . . . . None
Honours: . . . . . TWO-TIME JAPANESE KARTING CHAMPION

HOTTEST DRIVE: First test for Ligier
BIGGEST SETBACK: Having to step back to Formula Three for 1993
MOST LIKELY TO SAY: "Quoi?"
LEAST LIKELY TO SAY: "Mai, oui."

RISING SON: Shinji Nakano is the latest from the Japanese conveyor-belt

RICARDO ROSSET

Sophomore hopeful

Ricardo Rosset did not enjoy as much success as he would have liked in his first year of Formula One. Back for more, he is looking for points, this time with the new Lola team.

Ricardo Rosset could surprise a number of people in the tight-knit but not always far-sighted world of the Formula One paddock this year. For this serious and analytical Brazilian driver is a lot better than people gave himself credit for in his rookie Grand Prix season with the Footwork team in 1996. He fully expects to establish him with Lola in the 16 Grands Prix that make up his sophomore year.

Last season, Ricardo had to run very much as number two to team leader Jos Verstappen. In a team that is struggling to be competitive, being in the shadows is not the place to be. A glance at his results shows that his ninth place in his first ever Grand Prix, in Australia, was not beaten until he went one better in Hungary 11 races later, suggesting that little progress was made. However, Ricardo brought his car home eight times. It's certainly not a great record in 16 Grands Prix, but six of these retirements were beyond his control and it was four times more than the once highly rated Verstappen managed. For the record, the more competitive Dutchman's best finish was only two places higher.

Having signed for the new Lola team, Ricardo was hoping for more of a crack of the whip and certainly more testing than he had in 1996. He was buoyed at the close of last year with some encouraging testing mileage in the

Bridgestone-shod Footwork test car, and this extra time at the wheel will have helped him no end in focusing on his 1997 programme.

Learning his craft

Ricardo cut his teeth in karts and then Formula Ford in his native Brazil before contesting the Formula Opel Euroseries during 1992. Two fruitful seasons in the British Formula Three Championship followed, with his flashes of speed becoming more regular during the second year as he won once for Team AJS in a season dominated by Jan Magnussen and placed fifth overall.

TRACK NOTES

Nationality: . . . . BRAZILIAN
Born: . . . . 27 JULY, 1968,
. . . . SAO PAULO, BRAZIL
Teams: . . . . ARROWS 1996,
. . . . LOLA 1997

Career record

First Grand Prix start: . . . .
. . . . 1996 AUSTRALIAN GP
Grand Prix starts: 16
Grand Prix wins: . . . . None
(best result: eighth, 1996 Hungarian GP)
Poles: . . . . None
Fastest laps: . . . . None
Points: . . . . None
Honours: 1995 FORMULA 3000 RUNNER-UP

HOTTEST DRIVE: Winning first Formula 3000 race
BIGGEST SETBACK: Being taken out by Katayama in Canada last year
MOST LIKELY TO SAY: "I was feeling my way in 1996."
LEAST LIKELY TO SAY: "Footwork was a competitive team in 1996."

OPTIMISTIC FAILURE: Ricardo Rosset is looking to make up ground with Lola

What followed in 1995 when Ricardo moved to Formula 3000 was far in excess of what people expected, despite strong form in pre-season testing. For he won first time out for the Super Nova team and slotted in another win to end the season runner-up to his vastly more experienced team-mate Vincenzo Sospiri. Armed with access to family money that Sospiri could only dream of, Ricardo was able to graduate to Footwork, while Sospiri had to make do with the test seat at Benetton. But that's motor racing for you.

However, everything went wrong in March 1997 as Lola withdrew when the money ran out.

RALF SCHUMACHER

A chip off the old block?

Being brother to a two-time World Champion has its advantages, but Ralf Schumacher will have to prove in his first Formula One season with Jordan that he too possesses talent.

It takes just one glance to see that Ralf and Michael Schumacher share the same parentage. Best seen in profile, that trademark shovel chin is there. It couldn't be anyone else, even though the 21-year-old is taller than his older brother, with lighter-coloured hair.

Then there's the matter of his arrogance, which was legendary last year as Ralf and his cohorts vaulted over the swipe-card gates into the Formula One paddock. No pass: no entry, is the golden rule. Others would have been shot for less, but he was "a Schumacher so stand aside" he seemed to be saying. Someone must have told him that he was earning enemies before he'd as much as got himself a ride for 1997, because when it was announced at the Portuguese Grand Prix that he would

race for Jordan, he was an altogether more acceptable human being.

What we know of Ralf is that he is quick, and his first runs in a Formula One car, with McLaren last summer, were impressive. Even if he had the luxury of several days of testing at the circuit beforehand. And his hopes of pushing aside Mika Hakkinen and moving direct to a seat with the Mercedes-powered team were dashed when team boss Ron Dennis re-signed Hakkinen. If Mercedes wants this publicity magnet to drive for McLaren, it will have to wait.

Starting early

Like Michael before him, Ralf was charging around on karts at his father's karting circuit from the age his contemporaries were being given their first bicycles. Following Michael's progress through the junior formulae and on to Formula One gave Ralf an eye-opening education in the world of car racing. And, with his elder brother ensconced at Benetton for a second full season of Formula One, Ralf was finally old enough to race cars. He went directly to Formula Three, being a pace-setter in his first season. He drove for WTS Racing, the team owned by Willi Weber, Michael's mentor and manager. Right at the end of the season, he scored his first win, helping him to third place overall behind Jorg Muller and Alexander Wurz.

Ralf's second season boiled down to a straight fight with Argentinian driver Norberto Fontana, with Fontana taking the title thanks to scoring 10 wins to Ralf's three. This pair met up again in Formula Nippon (Japan's version of Formula 3000) last year, and Ralf was able to land the title at the final round, even though he crashed out and had to wait until shortly before

the end, when Le Mans Company team-mate Naoki Hattori also crashed and handed the title back to the German. Fontana ended up fifth overall. However, by then, Ralf already had a Formula One contract in his pocket, as the first of Jordan's new signings. And, as he met the Grand Prix press pack for the first time, he expected to be joined by Damon Hill for this season. How wrong he was.

FAMOUS PROFILE: Ralf Schumacher is one of a select group of Formula One brothers

TRACK NOTES

Nationality:	. . . . GERMAN
Born:	. . . . 30 JUNE, 1975,
	. . . . KERPEN, GERMANY
Teams:	. . . . JORDAN 1997

Career record

First Grand Prix start:	. . . .
	. . . . .1997 AUSTRALIAN GP
Grand Prix starts:	 2
Grand Prix wins:	. . . . None
Poles:	. . . . None
Fastest laps:	. . . . None
Points:	. . . . None

Honours: . . .1996 FORMULA NIPPON CHAMPION, 1995 GERMAN FORMULA THREE RUNNER-UP & 1995 MACAU FORMULA THREE GP WINNER

BIGGEST SETBACK: Not being as fast as his brother.
MOST LIKELY TO SAY: "Being a Schumacher opens doors, but to keep it open you have to be quick."
LEAST LIKELY TO SAY: "Please."

VINCENZO SOSPIRI

Bolt from the blue

Just when it looked as though Sospiri had missed the boat to Formula One, the former Formula 3000 Champion shot in from the flanks to claim the second Lola ride.

Vincenzo Sospiri is one of those drivers that no one ever thought would get to Formula One. Not because he wasn't good enough, but more because his face simply didn't seem to fit and he certainly didn't have sufficient family money behind him to ease his passage.

The Italian explained this lack of progress when he was in Formula 3000 as stemming from his father being a chicken farmer. And not even a very large one at that. However, just when his career appeared to have faltered, he came as if from nowhere to sprint past several more fancied drivers to grab the second Lola.

His team-mate is none other than Ricardo Rosset, Vincenzo's former colleague in the Super Nova team. But whereas the wealthy Brazilian went on to drive for Footwork in

1996, Vincenzo languished as a little-used test driver for Benetton. But then it all came right and Lola picked his services.

Chance of a lifetime

Sospiri is one of the most laid-back drivers in Formula One. When all around him is in turmoil, he looks calm. But, look a little closer, and you will find that he's quite a nervy individual, his laugh and devil-may-care attitude frequently masking other emotions.

Indeed, his manner has often infuriated those close to him, like those trying to tap the talent that made him the World Kart Champion in 1987. When he moved to racing cars, he took the unusual step for an Italian of turning his back on the Italian scene and racing in the

British Formula Ford series. And he flew from the outset, displaying a breathtaking talent. Victory in the end-of-year Formula Ford Festival capped a cracking first year. Two seasons of Formula Vauxhall followed with a relatively small budget. After wining the 1990 British title he went straight to Formula 3000, as team mate to Damon Hill. And no love was lost between this pair. Arriving finally in Formula One with Damon having already 21 Grand Prix victories will set Vincenzo's teeth on edge. But there was more frustration to follow, as the Lola was never likely to be able to challenge even midfield cars.

Sospiri's strongest suit, though, is his race-craft. Frequently almost disinterested in qualifying, he used to be seen tearing up the order. In Formula One, he will have to be interested every time he climbs into the cockpit. So, someone will have to nurture him, or a fine talent will never fulfil its potential.

After failing to qualify in Melbourne, Lola withdrew, this delaying Sospiri's debut further.

TRACK NOTES

Nationality: . . . . ITALIAN
Born: . . . . 7 OCTOBER, 1966
. . . . FORLI, ITALY
Teams: . . . . LOLA 1997

Career record
Grand Prix starts: . . . . None
Honours: . . 1995 FORMULA 3000 CHAMPION, 1990 VAUXHALL LOTUS CHAMPION, 1988 FORMULA FORD FESTIVAL WINNER, 1987 WORLD KART CHAMPION

AT LAST: It took laid-back Italian Vincenzo Sospiri a long time to graduate from the ranks of Formula 3000

JOS VERSTAPPEN

Dutch comet

Jos Verstappen burst on to Formula One like an explosion. He was wild, but quick. And he was with Benetton. That bubble has burst and he's now trying to rebuild his reputation at Tyrrell.

It's been too much too soon for Jos Verstappen. His rise to Formula One makes the description meteoric look pedestrian, for it took the young Dutchman little more than 50 races from his first car race to the day his Benetton was wheeled on to the grid for the 1994 Brazilian Grand Prix, as a replacement for the injured JJ Lehto. He had just turned 22 and his career was ahead of him. What came next was not so glorious and, three years later, he is older and wiser but no further on.

It's hard to say what went wrong, as Jos was forced out of his opening Grand Prix, lucky to survive flipping his car after colliding with Eddie Irvine's Jordan. He also retired in the next race, then had to stand down when Lehto returned and was only brought back mid-season when Lehto's comeback was adjudged unsuccessful.

Up in smoke

Then, in the German Grand Prix, Jos was engulfed in flames in the most ferocious pitlane fire ever. That he got away with minor burns was astonishing. That he could happily return for the next race, the Hungarian Grand Prix, and sit through further refuelling halts was incredible. And third place at the Hungaroring was just reward. A further third place in Belgium and fifth in Portugal showed he was matching guile with speed.

Jos moved to Simtek for 1995 and shone for the low-budget team, running sixth in Argentina before his gearbox packed up. But the team folded at Monaco and Jos was left without a drive. His return to Formula One with Footwork in 1996 was not covered in glory, with far too many occasions when Jos went bounding off through the gravel. Indeed, he failed to finish 12 of the 16 races, coming away

MOVING ON: Jos Verstappen has joined Mika Salo at Tyrrell for 1997

with just one sixth place and a suitably tarnished reputation.

Looking back at Jos's early career doesn't take much time, for after karts in which he won every title going in Holland and Belgium, he moved directly into Formula Opel in 1992, winning the Benelux title, as well as winning races in the European series. He won the 1993 German Formula Three title for the crack WTS Racing team. And, not only did he win eight times, but Jos also won the prestigious Marlboro Masters international Formula Three race on his home track at Zandvoort.

He spent the winter gaining experience in more powerful Formula Atlantic cars in New Zealand. However, before he headed south for the sunshine, he turned up at a Formula One test at Estoril and stunned onlookers by lapping a Footwork only fractionally slower than regular driver Derek Warwick had managed in qualifying for the Portuguese Grand Prix. On the strength of this, he was signed up as Benetton's test driver. When Lehto broke his neck in a testing accident at Silverstone, Jos was in for the first two Grands Prix. Yes, just two years on from his first car race.

TRACK NOTES

Nationality: . . . . DUTCH
Born: . . . . 4 MARCH, 1972,
. . . . MONTFORT, HOLLAND
Teams: . . . . BENETTON 1994,
. . . SIMTEK 1995, ARROWS 1996,
. . . . TYRRELL 1977

Career record

First Grand Prix start: . . . .
. . . . 1994 BRAZILIAN GP
Grand Prix starts: 33
Grand Prix wins: . . . . None
(best result: third, 1994 Hungarian GP
& 1994 Belgian GP)
Poles: . . . . None
Fastest laps: . . . . None
Points: 11
Honours: 1993 GERMAN FORMULA
THREE CHAMPION, 1992 BENELUX
FORMULA OPEL CHAMPION

**HOTTEST DRIVE: When he caught fire
in 1994 German Grand Prix.**
**BIGGEST SETBACK: Being pitched into
a flip at 1994 Brazilian Grand Prix.**
**MOST LIKELY TO SAY: "I will get it
right this year."**
**LEAST LIKELY TO SAY: "Briatore was
right to drop me from Benetton."**

THE TRACKS

Like the drivers, no two tracks are alike. From the opening race at Melbourne's Albert Park to the season closer at Estoril in Portugal, the drivers will once again be able to delight in racing at some great tracks — with Spa and Suzuka standing out.

Silverstone, Spa and Suzuka are all names to conjure with as great tracks that have hosted some of the best ever Grands Prix. They've seen Mansell go head-to-head with Piquet, Schumacher against Villeneuve and Prost versus Senna. And they mark some of the high points of the Formula One season.

The teams transport their high-tech kit tens of thousands of miles every year as the Grand Prix circus brings the world's mightiest show to town in 17 different locations in a busy week-on, week-off pattern. But which are the best tracks, the ones that set the drivers alive with anticipation? Which are the worst, the ones they'd rather pull their toenails out than visit or race on?

Despite recent homogenization in the name of safety, several tracks stand out as drivers' circuits, ones at which the top drivers can get stuck in and shine, even if they're not lucky enough to be driving one of the best cars. One such is Spa in Belgium. It sweeps through the forested Ardennes hills, with a lap long enough to get your teeth into. Television shots have a

habit of flattening inclines, but the track truly climbs and plunges. Just try walking up Eau Rouge, the most fearsome corner in modern day racing, and your calf muscles will soon be crying for a rest.

Monaco, likewise, is steeper than it looks on screen, and far narrower. It would be hard enough driving it alone, but when racing with 23 others you can never relax. Schumacher did last year and he crashed out of the race on the opening lap.

Many Britons make the annual pilgrimage to Silverstone, but it's not just the patriots who think it is a great track. Because of its wealth of history, dating back to the first modern-day Grand Prix race, held there in 1950, Silverstone is, without doubt, right up there with the greats of Formula One . Every year it appears to have a slightly different lay-out, but the safety backlash that emasculated some of the quicker bits – hurriedly installed in the wake of Ayrton Senna's tragic death during the San Marino Grand Prix at Imola in 1994 – are gradually being put back to the way they were: fast.

It's not just the application of safety measures that have changed the nature of the circuits. The modern Formula One car is a very different beast to its predecessors of even a decade ago, and the surge in technology has helped the driver rather then the spectator, with braking distances being slashed thanks to the introduction of carbon-fibre brakes. The problem is, most overtaking is done in the braking zone.

Then there are tracks that looks great on paper, like Hungary's twisty Hungaroring, but only something as small as a motorbike could find an overtaking line. A Formula One car? Forget it! However, the advent of fuel stops means that some drivers don't even try to overtake. Not Villeneuve, though. Remember the way he passed Schumacher on the outside around Estoril's slingshot last corner? It was epic and certainly caught the double World Champion by surprise.

OVER THE LIMIT: Michael Schumacher's Ferrari goes for a wild ride during the Brazilian Grand Prix at Interlagos

MELBOURNE

ROUND 1, 9 MARCH 1997

McLaren is back

David Coulthard's victorious season opener put McLaren back in the winner's circle for the first time since Ayrton Senna won in Australia in the final Grand Prix of 1993.

SUPER MAC: David Coulthard celebrates victory for McLaren in Melbourne – team-mate Mika Hakkinen came third

When the cars hit Melbourne's Albert Park track for the new season it was the first chance to see how well each team had done in developing its cars over the close-season. And, sadly for the other 11 teams, the new Williams-Renault FW19s seemed to have an even bigger advantage than in 1996. When championship favourite Jacques Villeneuve placed his on pole by the mammoth margin of over 1.75 seconds from new team-mate Heinz-Harald Frentzen, who was in turn 0.3 seconds up on Michael Schumacher's Ferrari, the writing was on the wall.

Unfortunately for the Canadian, life is never that simple, as he made a poor start and was tipped off into retirement at the first corner along with Johnny Herbert's fast-starting Sauber, courtesy of an over-ambitious dive down the inside by Ferrari driver Eddie Irvine.

Still, at least they got to take the start, which was more than reigning World Champion Damon Hill managed. Having endured endless problems with his Arrows, he scraped on to the grid in the dying moments of qualifying, as the 20th of the 22 starters. Then his car stopped on the parade lap when a throttle sensor failed. His reaction probably added a few new words to the Australian vocabulary.

And so Frentzen found himself out front, easing away to what looked to be a dream debut for Williams. But Coulthard, Schumacher and Mika Hakkinen in the second McLaren were going well, all relieved to have steered clear of that first corner accident, and right behind them the Benetton boys Jean Alesi and Gerhard Berger were motoring better than they had managed in qualifying.

Running a two-stop strategy, Frentzen appeared to have everything under control, even though he emerged behind Coulthard and Schumacher after his first stop. Unaccustomed to this position of having the race under control, though, the German failed to push sufficiently hard in the middle section of the race to have enough of an advantage so that after Coulthard and Schumacher made their one and only pitstops he would be able to make his second stop and emerge still in the lead. Realizing this, he upped the pace, but all this was undone when one of his wheels jammed during his second stop and he re-emerged third, five seconds adrift of Schumacher, who was two seconds down on Coulthard.

Now we had a race, and Frentzen soon caught Schumacher, making the first three run almost nose-to-tail. But Schumacher was forced to pit for more fuel six laps before the finish as a fault in his fuel rig hadn't allowed him to take on the correct amount when he first stopped.

This left Frentzen free to attack Coulthard. But, with three laps to go, Frentzen crashed when a front brake disc disintegrated, leaving Coulthard able to win as he pleased, triggering massive celebrations in the McLaren camp which were added to when Hakkinen chased Schumacher home, he in turn holding off Berger.

Alesi should have been part of this cluster, but he failed to come in for fuel when requested and ran out. Olivier Panis gave the Prost team (formerly Ligier) its first points for fifth, with Nicola Larini opening his account for Sauber in sixth.

And what of the rest? Well, the Jordan team failed to record a finish, but both rookie Ralf Schumacher and Giancarlo Fisichella showed a great turn of speed. So, things are looking up for Eddie Jordan's boys.

The new Stewart team also failed to get a car to the end, but the fact that Rubens Barrichello qualified 11th and was eighth when he parked up shows that Ford's new works team has promise indeed.

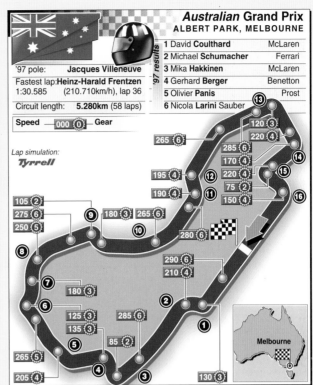

Australian Grand Prix
ALBERT PARK, MELBOURNE

1 David **Coulthard**	McLaren
2 Michael **Schumacher**	Ferrari
3 Mika **Hakkinen**	McLaren
4 Gerhard **Berger**	Benetton
5 Olivier **Panis**	Prost
6 Nicola **Larini** Sauber

'97 pole: Jacques Villeneuve

Fastest lap: Heinz-Harald Frentzen 1:30.585 (210.710km/h), lap 36

Circuit length: 5.280km (58 laps)

Speed 000 0 Gear

Lap simulation: *Tyrrell*

Melbourne

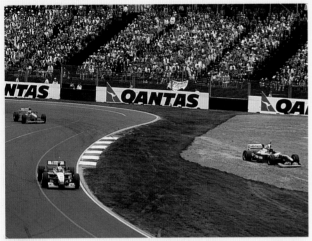

ONLY THE LONELY: Jacques Villeneuve's Williams sits abandoned on the grass after his first-lap exit as eventual winner David Coulthard (front) and Michael Schumacher speed past

1997 Race Results (After 58 Laps)

POS	DRIVER	TEAM	LAPS	TIME/RETIREMENT	GRID POS
1	David Coulthard	McLaren	58	1h30m28.718s	4
2	Michael Schumacher	Ferrari	58	1h30m48.764s	3
3	Mika Hakkinen	McLaren	58	1h30m50.895s	6
4	Gerhard Berger	Benetton	58	1h30m51.559s	10
5	Olivier Panis	Prost	58	1h31m29.026s	9
6	Nicola Larini	Sauber	58	1h32m04.758s	13
7	Shinji Nakano	Prost	56		16
8	Heinz-Harald Frentzen	Williams	55	Accident	2
9	Jarno Trulli	Minardi	55		17
10	Pedro Diniz	Arrows	54		22
R	Rubens Barrichello	Stewart	49	Engine	11
R	Mika Salo	Tyrrell	42	Electrics	18
R	Jan Magnussen	Stewart	36	Suspension	19
R	Jean Alesi	Benetton	34	Ran out of fuel	8
R	Ukyo Katayama	Minardi	32	Fuel feed	15
R	Giancarlo Fisichella	Jordan	14	Accident	14
R	Jos Verstappen	Tyrrell	2	Accident	21
R	Ralf Schumacher	Jordan	1	Driveshaft	12
R	Eddie Irvine	Ferrari	0	Accident damage	5
R	Jacques Villeneuve	Williams	0	Accident	1
R	Johnny Herbert	Sauber	0	Accident	7
NS	Damon Hill	Arrows	0	Throttle sensor	20
NQ	Vincenzo Sospiri	Lola	–	–	–
NQ	Ricardo Rosset	Lola	–	–	–

Fastest lap: Heinz-Harald Frentzen 1m30.585s (130.935mph/210.710km/h).
Weather conditions: Hot and sunny for qualifying, warm and cloudy for the race, 23C.

INTERLAGOS

ROUND 2, 30 MARCH 1997

Villeneuve makes his mark

Jacques Villeneuve's championship bid started in Sao Paulo, coming good after the disappointment of Melbourne. But Benetton's Gerhard Berger was not far behind at flagfall.

Everyone expected Williams, and lead driver Jacques Villeneuve in particular, to dominate proceedings in 1997. And so it proved in the Brazilian Grand Prix at Interlagos, from start to finish.

As at Melbourne's Albert Park, the French-Canadian slotted his Renault-powered Williams FW19 on pole, making his rivals look second rate. But this time it was rather closer, as he was just half a second clear of the second driver, this time Ferrari's Michael Schumacher. And from here back it was incredibly close, with Gerhard Berger (Benetton), Mika Hakkinen (McLaren), Olivier Panis (Prost) and Jean Alesi (Benetton) just a blink of an eye slower on their best qualifying laps. Australian Grand Prix winner David Coulthard couldn't find a sensible balance on his McLaren over the notorious bumps and was 12th, three places behind none other than Damon Hill who was far happier with his Arrows than he had been at the previous race.

Villeneuve only made one mistake all weekend, and that was to be slow off the line, as he had been in Australia. And this let Schumacher lead into the first corner. But Villeneuve found himself out on the dirty line and speared across the grass on the exit of the first corner, rejoining at the foot of the hill by the exit of the second corner well down the order as cars speared in all directions behind as Giancarlo Fisichella spun his Jordan in the pack. But, salvation, the red flag was hung out and the race stopped as Rubens Barrichello's Stewart was beached dangerously on the start line having stalled.

At the second time of asking, Villeneuve got it all right and led away. This time he made no mistakes and pulled away at an amazing rate. Indeed, after less than 10 laps he was fully 10 seconds clear and would only be headed when he called in for his two scheduled pitstops.

On this occasion, Benetton proved that it was back on the right track and it was Berger who rose from the ranks to offer the sternest challenge. Initially behind Hakkinen, he soon moved up to third then reeled in and passed Schumacher. Once second, the Austrian veteran started to chip away at Villeneuve's lead. The gap came down to as low as 4.1 seconds with 10 laps to run, but he realized that he was never going to catch the Williams, and opted to simply run to the finish and collect the six points for second place.

NORMAL SERVICE IS RESUMED: Jacques Villeneuve took advantage of a restart to dominate the race in Brazil

The smile on Benetton team boss Flavio Briatore's face was even larger when team-mate Alesi paid attention to his pit boards and pitted twice en route to sixth place.

Although Villeneuve had driven beautifully to lay down his challenge for the 1997 drivers' title, and Berger's aggressive charge to second showed Benetton is back, in many ways the drive of the race came from Olivier Panis. Fifth in Melbourne for the Prost team, he went two places better to be third at Interlagos, again adopting a one-stop strategy and proving that the Bridgestone tyres can go a greater distance than their Goodyear rivals without degrading. Indeed, when his rivals called for their first stops, he rose as high as second. Hill, also on Bridgestones, used a similar strategy to climb as high as fourth. Hill was later to hit trouble and fall back, but the French driver kept pressing on and finished easily clear of a tight bunch of Hakkinen, Schumacher and Alesi, all of whom pitted twice.

Johnny Herbert had a troubled weekend, but raced well to climb to seventh in the lead Sauber, while Fisichella came home eighth. Ninth place went to Frentzen, and the best thing that can be said about his weekend was that he remained unlapped. He clearly will have to go better to keep his seat at Williams.

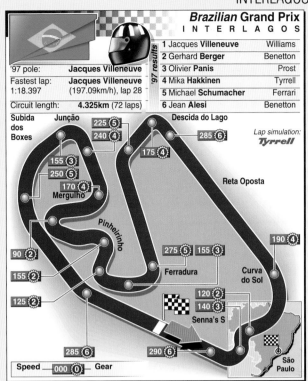

Brazilian Grand Prix
I N T E R L A G O S

	'97 results	
1	Jacques **Villeneuve**	Williams
2	Gerhard **Berger**	Benetton
3	Olivier **Panis**	Prost
4	Mika **Hakkinen**	Tyrrell
5	Michael **Schumacher**	Ferrari
6	Jean **Alesi**	Benetton

'97 pole: **Jacques Villeneuve**
Fastest lap: **Jacques Villeneuve**
1:18.397 (197.09km/h), lap 28
Circuit length: **4.325km** (72 laps)

Lap simulation: **Tyrrell**

Subida dos Boxes · Junção · Descida do Lago · Reta Oposta · Mergulho · Pinheirinho · Ferradura · Curva do Sol · Senna's S · São Paulo

Speed — 000 (0) — Gear

NOWHERE TO GO: The first corner chaos claimed only Jan Magnussen's Stewart, but it was his team-mate Rubens Barrichello who brought out the red flag by stalling on the start line. The Brazilian driver took the spare car for the restart

1997 Race Results (After 72 Laps)

POS	DRIVER	TEAM	LAPS	TIME/RETIREMENT	GRID POS
1	Jacques Villeneuve	Williams	72	1h36m06.99s	1
2	Gerhard Berger	Benetton	72	1h36m11.18s	3
3	Olivier Panis	Prost	72	1h36m22.86s	5
4	Mika Hakkinen	McLaren	72	1h36m40.02s	4
5	Michael Schumacher	Ferrari	72	1h36m40.72s	2
6	Jean Alesi	Benetton	72	1h36m41.01s	6
7	Johnny Herbert	Sauber	72	1h36m57.90s	13
8	Giancarlo Fisichella	Jordan	72	1h37m07.63s	7
9	Heinz-Harald Frentzen	Williams	72	1h37m22.39s	8
10	David Coulthard	McLaren	71		12
11	Nicola Larini	Sauber	71		19
12	Jarno Trulli	Minardi	71		17
13	Mika Salo	Tyrrell	71		22
14	Shinji Nakano	Prost	71		15
15	Jos Verstappen	Tyrrell	70		21
16	Eddie Irvine	Ferrari	70		14
17	Damon Hill	Arrows	68	Engine fire	9
18	Ukyo Katayama	Minardi	67		18
R	Ralf Schumacher	Jordan	52	Electrics	10
R	Rubens Barrichello	Stewart	16	Suspension	11
R	Pedro Diniz	Arrows	15	Spin	16
R	Jan Magnussen	Stewart	0	Accident damage	20

Fastest lap: Jacques Villeneuve in 1m18.397s (122.47mph/197.09km/h).
Weather conditions: Qualifying hot and sunny. Race overcast and warm, 20C.

BUENOS AIRES

ROUND 3, 13 APRIL 1997

The current Buenos Aires circuit lay-out is too twisty and slow to be a classic. This is a shame because the original circuit was a mighty one with plenty of high-speed sweepers.

A lap of the circuit in its current guise is a stop-and-go procedure, with drivers having to be careful at the unimaginatively named first corner, Curva Numero Uno, for this is a tightening right-hander. And, even though the track and the grass verges are wide, there can be trouble there, as was witnessed in 1995 when Jean Alesi locked up, spinning into the middle of the pack with costly consequences.

Keep it clean through there though, and the drivers run through a fourth-gear kink into a left-hand hairpin. Up through the gearbox from second, there's a left, then a long right on to the back straight. This pours into the sixth-gear Ascari bend, the best on the track taken at over 170mph. Another second-gear hairpin follows, then a double-apex left, the Senna esses (a tight left and a tighter right), and finally the tight Horquilla right-hander on to the pit straight. No wonder some drivers refer to it as a glorified kart track. However, not one of them can complain about visiting Buenos Aires, for it is one of the most stunning cities in the world.

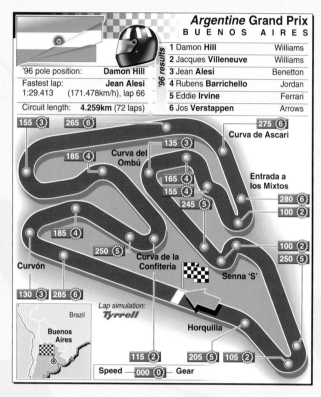

Argentine Grand Prix
B U E N O S   A I R E S

'96 pole position: **Damon Hill**
Fastest lap: **Jean Alesi**
1:29.413   (171.478km/h), lap 66
Circuit length: **4.259km** (72 laps)

'96 results		
1 Damon **Hill**	Williams
2 Jacques **Villeneuve**	Williams
3 Jean **Alesi**	Benetton
4 Rubens **Barrichello**	Jordan
5 Eddie **Irvine**	Ferrari
6 Jos **Verstappen**	Arrows

Curva de Ascari
Curva del Ombú
Entrada a los Mixtos
Curvón
Curva de la Confiteria
Senna 'S'
Horquilla

Brazil
Buenos Aires

Lap simulation: *Tyrrell*

Speed — 000 0 — Gear

EASY ENTRY, TRICKY EXIT: Curva Numero Uno catches many out with its tightening radius

Welcome home

Argentina has only just returned to the Formula One calendar after years in the wilderness. Home of the likes of five-time World Champion Juan Manuel Fangio and Froilan Gonzales, the country was a hub of world motor racing in the 1950s, with Fangio drawing in hundreds of thousands of fans on what they hoped would be a triumphant homecoming in 1953. On that occasion it didn't work, but he won the race on the next four occasions and the race remained on the calendar until 1960, with the exception of 1959.

However, by then, its trickle of talent to Europe dried up and the race was not held again until 1972, when local driver Carlos Reutemann took pole in his Brabham but couldn't stop Jackie Stewart from winning in his Tyrrell. With the exception of 1976, when political unrest led to its cancellation, the race ran until 1981, usually as the season-opener in a two-race package with the Brazilian. To the crowd's disappointment, Reutemann was destined never to win the Argentinian Grand Prix, with second place in 1979 and 1981 his best results.

It was only in 1995 that the Formula One circus revisited Argentina, sadly to a less demanding track. Still, Damon Hill clearly loves it, as he has won there two years on the trot for Williams. With Reutemann now a state senator, the future of the race looks secure, and there are a host of Argentinian drivers lining up for a crack at Formula One, each one hoping to become a latter-day Reutemann.

IMOLA

ROUND 4, 27 APRIL 1997

Imola remains one of the best circuits to visit. The viewing is good, the atmosphere is great and the food magnificent. And if the Ferraris win, then the nearby town really will be painted red. However, this parkland track will always be remembered as the one that claimed the lives of Ayrton Senna and rookie Roland Ratzenberger on the same weekend in 1994.

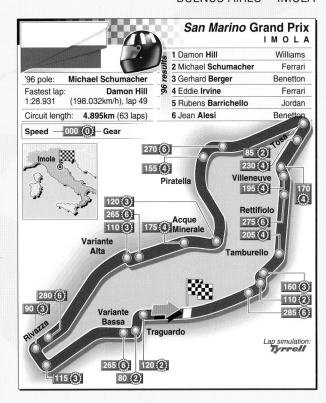

San Marino Grand Prix
IMOLA

1	Damon **Hill**	Williams
2	Michael **Schumacher**	Ferrari
3	Gerhard **Berger**	Benetton
4	Eddie **Irvine**	Ferrari
5	Rubens **Barrichello**	Jordan
6	Jean **Alesi**	Benetton

'96 pole: **Michael Schumacher**

Fastest lap: **Damon Hill**
1:28.931 (198.032km/h), lap 49

Circuit length: **4.895km (63 laps)**

Speed ——000—0—Gear

Lap simulation: *Tyrrell*

A lap of the track offers all sorts of delights as the ribbon of tarmac threads its way along the banks of a river, through a series of kinks that made it almost a flat-out blast from Rivazza, past the pits, to the Tosa hairpin, via the Tamburello and Villeneuve kinks. Since that doubly-tragic weekend in 1994, a chicane has been inserted at Tamburello and another before Villeneuve, while the Variante Bassa before the pits has been made less extreme.

From the hard left at Tosa, the track climbs sharply to the left-hander at Piratella that crests the wooded hilltop. Then the track dives down to the Acque Minerale right-hander before climbing again to the chicane at Variante Alta from where it drops back to the level of the startline, via the double-apex left-hander called Rivazza.

Imola is a circuit with enough tight corners and chicanes to cook the brakes, wear out the tyres and burst transmissions, but it's still a fine track. It's not as fast as it was, and it's lost the best of its rhythm, but passing is still a possibility, which is more than can be said of some circuits.

Visit Imola, and you come away in no doubt that only one team counts as far as the fans are concerned: Ferrari. Indeed, old man Ferrari, Enzo to his mother, had the circuit named after his son Dino, who died tragically young.

Double Italian

It seems as though the circuit has always held a Grand Prix, but it was only as recently as 1980 that it was given the go-ahead. Since 1981 it has had a Grand Prix at the start of the year, with the Grand Prix at Monza traditionally slated for the tail-end of the season. So, how come Italy gets two Grands Prix a year, while other countries have to make do with one? Because the race at Imola is known as the San Marino Grand Prix, named after the nearby principality, the one that always get thrashed at football. Races at Imola are famous for cars expiring or even running out of fuel in the closing laps, as used to happen when the engines were turbocharged and thirsty, and no-one made fuel stops. However, it's also famous for big shunts, as experienced by Nelson Piquet at Tamburello in 1987 and Gerhard Berger at the same corner two years later. But, the darkest day ever for Ferrari fans came in 1991 when Alain Prost spun one of their beloved red cars off on the parade lap, and then Jean Alesi ran out of road three laps later in the other.

GLORIOUS SETTING: Imola's flowing circuit dips through the wonderful parkland setting. This is the revised Villeneuve chicane

MONACO

ROUND 5, 11 MAY 1997

It should have been removed from the Formula One calendar years ago, as the track is too narrow and bumpy for racing. Indeed, the race is an anachronism. But the sponsors love it, and it gives Formula One some sorely needed glamour as the cars stream past the casinos and the yachts of the rich and the famous.

Blink when racing a lap of Monaco and your car will be in the barriers, which are never more than a metre or so from the racing line. Starting at the grid: to confuse matters it isn't even on a straight piece of road, but on one that curves right towards the first corner, Ste Devote. This really is a tight right-hander. If it was wider, it would be fine, but it's so narrow that there is only one line around it, which always leads to trouble at the start as the drivers try to take it two- or even three-abreast. Or, in the case of Derek Daly back in 1980, in the air, as he clipped a car ahead, vaulted over it, bounced once and then landed on his Tyrrell team-mate Jean-Pierre Jarier. So, caution is required – if rarely applied – here.

HARD ON THE BRAKES: And nowhere more so than on the entry to the famous Loews hairpin

Then it's up the hill towards Casino Square, minding not to lose control on the white lines, as Nigel Mansell did when leading in 1984 (Drivers' Book of Excuses, Chapter 10). The left-hander into Casino Square is blind over the crest of the hill, and a driver has to set his car up unsighted for the right-hander that runs out of the far side of the square and down past the famed Tip-Top Bar to the Mirabeau hairpin. A street circuit like no other, drivers can even hook a wheel over the pavement on the inside of the corner. The famous Loews hairpin is next and it's not an overtaking place, but every year people try, simply fed up with being unable to pass anywhere else.

Tunnel trouble

Then there's the double-right on to the sea front at Portier, the first part of which Michael Schumacher failed to negotiate on the opening lap in 1996. Then comes the most difficult piece of track; the tunnel. To make matters all the trickier, it's not straight through there, but a long right-hand arc. Out of the tunnel, blinking in the daylight, drivers have to hit the anchors and jink left, right, left on to the harbourside. Careering past yachts whose decks are filled with people who look as though they've strolled off the set of *The Long Good Friday*, the drivers have to steel themselves for the fast left at Tabac and funnel their cars left, right, right, left around Piscine and then finally jink into the La Rascasse hairpin, and plant their right foot to get the power down again for another lap. Easy it isn't.

Nelson Piquet once described driving at speed around Monaco as like riding a bicycle around your sitting room. It's no wonder a race win here is worth two anywhere else.

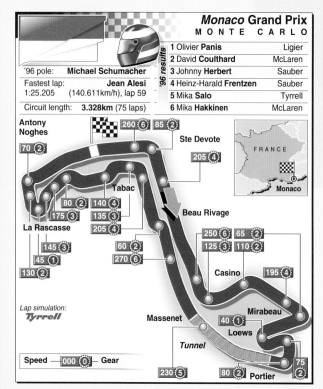

Monaco Grand Prix
MONTE CARLO

'96 results		
1 Olivier **Panis**		Ligier
2 David **Coulthard**		McLaren
3 Johnny **Herbert**		Sauber
4 Heinz-Harald **Frentzen**		Sauber
5 Mika **Salo**		Tyrrell
6 Mika **Hakkinen**		McLaren

'96 pole: **Michael Schumacher**
Fastest lap: **Jean Alesi**
1:25.205 (140.611km/h), lap 59
Circuit length: **3.328km (75 laps)**

Antony Noghes

Ste Devote

FRANCE

Monaco

Tabac

Beau Rivage

La Rascasse

Casino

Lap simulation:
Tyrrell

Massenet

Mirabeau

Loews

Tunnel

Speed — 000 0 — Gear

Portier

BARCELONA

ROUND 6, 25 MAY 1997

Spain has two Grand Prix circuits: Catalunya just outside Barcelona and Jerez in the south. Both are "modern" circuits, meaning they have a mixture of fast and slow corners. Both ought to have good weather, although Catalunya has produced more than its share of rain.

Despite having never produced a top-line Formula One driver, Spain has a long history of hosting Grands Prix, and five circuits have shared the honour. The round-the-houses Pedralbes circuit on the outskirts of Barcelona was the first in the early 1950s. But then Spain didn't have another Grand Prix until the Jarama circuit near Madrid took over in 1968. A year later, the Montjuich Park circuit in a park in Barcelona took its turn in an alternating pattern that continued until 1975 when the rear wing came off Rolf Stommelen's car, it vaulted the barrier and killed five spectators. Since then, the race has been shared by Catalunya and Jerez.

The Catalunya circuit is now established as the home of the Spanish Grand Prix. Built at the start of the 1990s, it is better than other modern circuits in that the designer has taken into account the fact that people like to watch overtaking rather than processions, and has designed it so that the long main straight leads into a sharp corner and thus requires heavy braking. And this is exactly where overtaking happens.

This first corner, Elf, is a right followed by a left and then there's a long uphill right-hander. Get this right in fifth gear and a driver will be flying before hitting the brakes for the Repsol right-hander. From this point the track dips down and feeds through the Seat left-hander, through a left kink and into the uphill left-hander that takes one up to the Campsa corner at the crest of the hill. Then, carrying as much speed as possible over the crest, it's time to go downhill again, and drivers hit roughly 170mph down the back straight, before the tight left at La Caixa and the start of the climb back up to Banc Sabadell corner. The final two bends are crucial to a quick lap time, as they're fast, fifth-gear corners on to the main straight.

Jerez is at the far end of the country, south of Seville. Dry and dusty, it is beautifully equipped, but too far from major cities to draw a crowd. The track is twisty, especially after the introduction of a chicane following Martin Donnelly's career-ending shunt at the Curva Ferrari behind the pits. But its principal claim to fame may be that it produced the second closest Grand Prix finish ever in 1986, when Ayrton Senna edged out Nigel Mansell by 0.014 seconds after almost 200 miles.

WHICH ONE'S THIS? Drivers have to work hard at Barcelona with a host of interesting corners

111

MONTREAL

ROUND 7, 15 JUNE 1997

Situated on an island in the St Lawrence River in Montreal, the circuit is built on the site of the old Expo 67 pavilions and every year it sends car after car into retirement, as the bumps and the tight corners stress the cars' moving parts like nowhere else.

Canada had a Grand Prix from the mid-1960s. Then it had Gilles Villeneuve. And now it has his son, Jacques Villeneuve. However, apart from minority interest in Formula One and the country's early Grands Prix, the Canadian populace remained more interested in snowmobile racing. That was until Gilles came along and won their hearts, as he took on the world in the most flamboyant style possible. Gilles died at Zolder qualifying for the 1982 Belgian Grand Prix, and Canada lost interest again, looking more to North America's indigenous IndyCar racing. But then Jacques arrived, won the IndyCar title and headed for Formula One. The premium on grandstand seats was never as great as it was last year, when everyone in Quebec, it seemed, wanted to see Jacques win on the

HARD RIGHT: The Montreal circuit offers two hairpins, numerous esses and a lengthy straight

circuit named after his father. He came close in 1996, but could do nothing to stop team-mate Damon Hill from beating him.

Sprinter's delight

And what a circuit the Circuit Gilles Villeneuve is. Or, more to the point, was. Prior to the insertion of chicanes that hit the world's circuits like a rash in the early 1990s. Running around the Olympic rowing basin and yet pinned in on two sides by the river, there's very little space for the track and even less for the grandstands. The sprint from the grid to the first corner always sees excited jockeying for position as the track goes tight left and then into a right-hand hairpin, the Virage Senna. And inevitably someone will get this wrong and bounce into the cars near by.

From there, drivers must negotiate a series of esses and chicanes before the curving back straight, all surrounded by temporary concrete barriers. After yet another chicane, comes the Pits Hairpin, the best overtaking spot, where Nigel Mansell waved to the fans on the final lap in 1991, only to stall and let Nelson Piquet through to win. The blast back to the start line is taken in top – sixth – with 180mph on the clock before the final chicane on to the start straight. Not surprisingly, with its stop-start nature, the circuit is known as a car-breaker.

The first Grands Prix were not held in Montreal, but variously at Mosport Park in Ontario and Quebec's Mont Tremblant. These races were always held in autumn and it was always a wonder to behold the colour of the leaves, making the backdrop one of the most attractive on the racing calendar. With the arrival of Gilles in Formula One, the Canadians had a front-runner to cheer and the race was moved to its current Montreal venue, with Gilles winning the first race there in 1978.

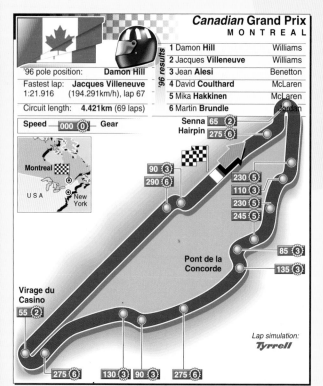

Canadian Grand Prix
MONTREAL

'96 results

1	Damon **Hill**	Williams
2	Jacques **Villeneuve**	Williams
3	Jean **Alesi**	Benetton
4	David **Coulthard**	McLaren
5	Mika **Hakkinen**	McLaren
6	Martin **Brundle**	Jordan

'96 pole position: **Damon Hill**

Fastest lap: **Jacques Villeneuve**
1:21.916 (194.291km/h), lap 67

Circuit length: **4.421km (69 laps)**

Speed ⎯ 000 ⓪ ⎯ Gear

Senna Hairpin 65 ②
275 ⑥

90 ③
290 ⑥

230 ⑤
110 ③
230 ⑤
245 ⑤

Montreal

USA New York

85 ③

Pont de la Concorde

135 ③

Virage du Casino

55 ②

Lap simulation:
Tyrrell

275 ⑥ 130 ③ 90 ③ 275 ⑥

MAGNY-COURS

ROUND 8, 29 JUNE 1997

Magny-Cours is nobody's favourite circuit. It is fine for the smaller categories of racing cars, with the Adelaide hairpin at the end of the back straight a great passing point. But, for Formula One, it's a case of "after you Claude!"

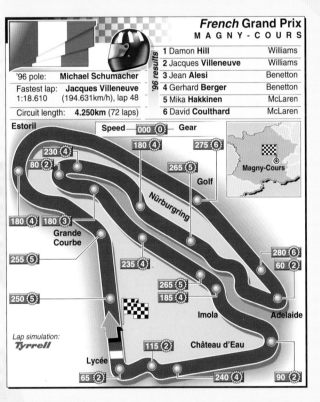

French Grand Prix
MAGNY-COURS

'96 results

1 Damon **Hill**		Williams
2 Jacques **Villeneuve**		Williams
3 Jean **Alesi**		Benetton
4 Gerhard **Berger**		Benetton
5 Mika **Hakkinen**		McLaren
6 David **Coulthard**		McLaren

'96 pole: **Michael Schumacher**
Fastest lap: **Jacques Villeneuve**
1:18.610 (194.631km/h), lap 48
Circuit length: **4.250km** (72 laps)

Speed —— 000 (0) —— Gear

Estoril
Golf
Nürburgring
Grande Courbe
Imola
Adelaide
Château d'Eau
Lycée

Lap simulation:
Tyrrell

For France, a country with perhaps a stronger and richer racing history than any other, having been home to the first ever motor race, back in 1894, when there was a race along public roads from Paris to Rouen, to have such a lacklustre circuit as Magny-Cours as its showpiece is a travesty. This happened when the country's president (Mitterand) wanted to help promote an otherwise backward, rural area. In an instant, the erstwhile club circuit was transformed and elevated into the centre of technical excellence of French motor sport. So, despite no one wanting to go there, it has been the home of the French Grand Prix since 1991.

The best of the lap at Magny-Cours comes right at the start, with the combination of the tightening Grande Courbe left-hander flowing into the long Estoril right-hander. It's essential to get this just right for a quick exit on to the back straight, as this leads into the principal overtaking point on the whole track: the Adelaide hairpin at the top of the hill. After

this ultra-tight right-hander, the track twists down through the Nurburgring esse, where Michael Schumacher pulled off on the parade lap last year, to the 180° hairpin. Then it's uphill again through the very fast Imola esses into the Chateau d'Eau right-hander and the drop down to the track's tightest chicane that precedes the tight Lycee, on to the start straight, that sees so many drivers all but kiss the pit wall as they get the power down on the exit.

The cost of modernizing

The tracks that went before it, though, have lagged behind modern-day Formula One requirements, rather like Brands Hatch has in England. If a country loses its Grand Prix, the revenue to keep up with developments is lost too. Reims was the first French venue to hold a modern (post-1950) Grand Prix on its almost triangular course, made up of public roads. In the same period, from the early 1950s to the late 1960s, a trickier track through the trees just outside Rouen was used intermittently, complete with a cobbled hairpin. However, perhaps the greatest track to have hosted the French Grand Prix was used next. High on the hill above Clermont-Ferrand in the Massif Central, dipping and twisting through a series of fast and often blind corners, it was a classic. But it was considered too dangerous as the cars became ever faster and the drivers decided that they would like to live to see another Christmas. So, the flat and fast Paul Ricard circuit in the south of France took over, with occasional forays to the tighter and hilly Dijon-Prenois circuit, before Magny-Cours took over.

END OF THE LAP: Jacques Villenueve enters Lycee, the final corner of the unpopular Magny-Cours circuit

SILVERSTONE

ROUND 9, 13 JULY 1997

Silverstone was once an airfield, although it's easy not to notice its origins these days, except that it's flat and open. And there are great places to watch.

Silverstone calls itself the "Home of British Motor Racing". In fact, it's more than that: it's one of the cradles of world motor sport.

A lap starts with the constantly changing Copse corner. Chopped in format after Ayrton Senna's death, it was opened out again prior to last year's race, and is now taken at around 100mph in fourth gear, before the drivers grab fifth then sixth, as they jink through Maggotts and dive into the Becketts esses. This is the most exhilarating part of the track, as it's very fast, yet offers a constant change of direction as it dives right, flicks left and then right again. Then it's hard on the power through the Chapel kink and on to the Hangar Straight and up to 180mph, before throwing out the anchors and hauling the car down to a speed that will let the driver turn into the Vale dip after Stowe. Hard left at the end of this, then right through the double-apex Club corner and up to sixth before another of the new corners: the Abbey chicane.

Originally the fastest corner, this is now very tight and it slows drivers before they reach Bridge, which remains a daunting corner as the

THEY'RE WATCHING YOU! The British Grand Prix is one of the best-attended races on the calendar

cars dive into a dip and then turn hard right, firing up into the infield section. This bit is fiddly, but it gives a good chance to gauge how close cars are to each other as the track meanders back and forth in front of the grandstands. Left at Priory, left at Brooklands, then twice right through the Luffields and once more through the Woodcote kink and the lap is complete. It doesn't flow as it used to, but the circuit owners are doing their best to give it back some of its old rhythm.

The early days

Designating the British Grand Prix only to Silverstone is a little misleading, as the race was held at Donington Park near Derby in the 1930s, when the mighty Mercedes and Auto Union teams came over and wiped the floor with the British "opposition". However, that was in the days before there was a Wolrd Championship.

Formula One started to take off in the 1950s, with the British trying everything they knew to break the Italian/German stranglehold: Alfa Romeo's initial domination was followed by Ferrari and Mercedes controlling the game. However, when the first British win came in 1955, it was not in a British-built car, but a Mercedes, and it was not at Silverstone, but up the road at Aintree, the home of the Grand National horse race, with the track running around the perimeter. The grandstands were filled to the rafters when Stirling Moss edged out team-mate Fangio to take the chequered flag.

The British Grand Prix alternated between Aintree and Silverstone until 1962, when Aintree hosted the race for the second year on the trot. But that was to be its last shot – the undulating Brands Hatch circuit in Kent took over alternate duties with Silverstone running from 1964 to 1986, since when its always been at Silverstone.

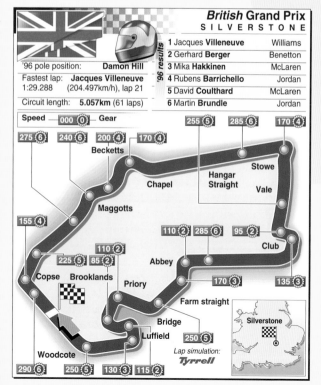

British Grand Prix
SILVERSTONE

'96 results		
1 Jacques **Villeneuve**	Williams
2 Gerhard **Berger**	Benetton
3 Mika **Hakkinen**	McLaren
4 Rubens **Barrichello**	Jordan
5 David **Coulthard**	McLaren
6 Martin **Brundle**	Jordan

'96 pole position: **Damon Hill**

Fastest lap: **Jacques Villeneuve**
1:29.288 (204.497km/h), lap 21

Circuit length: **5.057km** (61 laps)

Lap simulation: *Tyrrell*

HOCKENHEIM

ROUND 10, 27 JULY 1997

In character, Hockenheim is two different circuits: there's the twisty bit past the grandstands, and then there's the flat-out, 200mph plus blast through the trees, with just three chicanes to keep the drivers awake.

With every passing year, the memory of Jim Clark recedes slightly, but to many, Hockenheim will always be remembered as the place where the great British World Champion perished in an inconsequential Formula Two race at the start of 1968, shortly after he'd won his second World Championship for Lotus.

The track hasn't changed much since then. The first corner is a fast right-hander, where Damon Hill fell off when leading on the second lap in 1995. Then it's a blast up to the first chicane, the Jim Clark Kurve, trying not to let the car behind get a tow. A quick right and a left, and it's back on the gas to the far end of the loop and the Ost Kurve chicane. Then a twisting right on to another straight down to the third chicane. Known as the Ayrton Senna Kurve, this differs in that it's left then right. The cars remain out of sight until they burst back out of the trees at Agip

INTO THE INFIELD: Berger leads Benetton team mate Alesi into the Sachs Kurve at the end of the opening lap in 1996

Kurve and arrive back into the infield. Some passing moves are pulled off at Agip, but many prefer to dive past into the left-handed Sachs Kurve. There's a kink and then a double-apex right on to the start straight. It's a good track for slipstreaming, but it was so much better in the days before chicanes when the entire loop was flat-out with a slight lift for the Ost Kurve.

Nostalgia for the Nurburgring

The German Grand Prix hasn't always been held at Hockenheim. Indeed, with only two exceptions, it was held at the Nurburgring from 1951 to 1976. And the Nurburgring is a track that still makes older fans dewy-eyed. At over 14 miles in length, it offered more than a hundred corners, with points where the cars would become airborne and others where they would have to fight to stay within the confines of banked corners. Sadly, fans and drivers were shaken out of their reverie when Niki Lauda nearly lost his life there in 1976. Spectacular, yes, safe, no.

The two years in that period when the race went elsewhere were 1959, when it was held at the Avus circuit in Berlin, where two banked corners were joined by two enormously long straights. And the other occasion was in 1970 when it had its first foray to Hockenheim.

In 1985, the Grand Prix gave Hockenheim a miss, however, and the race returned to the Nurburgring. Not to the Nordschleife, though, but to a modern circuit built around the old pits. With its constant radius corners and grandstands set back a long way behind huge gravel traps and even larger grass verges, the circuit lost its great atmosphere. However, with the advent of "Schumachermania", it was swiftly brought back on to the calendar for 1995 and 1996 when it hosted European Grands Prix.

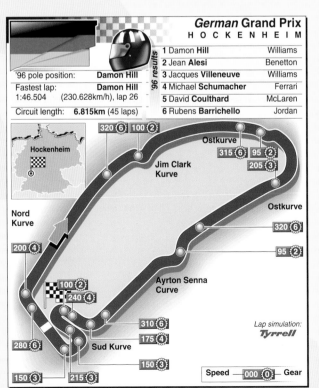

German Grand Prix
H O C K E N H E I M

'96 pole position: **Damon Hill**
Fastest lap: **Damon Hill**
1:46.504 (230.628km/h), lap 26
Circuit length: **6.815km (45 laps)**

'96 results		
1 Damon **Hill**	Williams
2 Jean **Alesi**	Benetton
3 Jacques **Villeneuve**	Williams
4 Michael **Schumacher**	Ferrari
5 David **Coulthard**	McLaren
6 Rubens **Barrichello**	Jordan

Lap simulation: *Tyrrell*

Speed —— 000 0 — Gear

HUNGARORING

ROUND 11, 10 AUGUST 1997

Set in undulating countryside with natural banking to offer the droves of spectators a stunning view of much of the track. Sadly, the Hungaroring is simply too tight and twisty to offer them any overtaking to watch.

Back in the 1970s, the thought of a Grand Prix taking place in an Eastern European country such as Hungary would have been preposterous. However, with the politics of the region changing at a raging pace as communism retreated, Hungary had its Grand Prix by 1986. They had a circuit purpose-built in rolling countryside, just outside capital city Budapest, for the occasion: the Hungaroring.

Situated in a wooded valley, the circuit makes the most of the natural terrain in that it spans the two sides of the valley and the dip in between, offering fantastic views from almost every vantage point.

The start/finish straight runs level with the slope on one side of the valley and feeds into a tight right-hander that drops in gradient from entry to exit as it doubles back on itself. A downhill left-hander follows before a dipping right that takes the drivers on to a straight that precedes to the bottom of the valley, before climbing up the other side and kinking left through Turn Four. The right-hander at the top puts the cars on to a level with the start straight on the far side of the valley, but the track is much twistier as it jinks right and left along the valley side until it reaches Turn Ten and drops down to Turn Eleven. From here, it climbs all the way up through to the final corner, a long right-hander that opens on to the main straight. A good exit speed here is essential if a driver wants to get into the slipstream of the car ahead, down the straight for a potential passing move into the first corner. Bumps are a problem and have caught out many drivers over the years.

Slow and stormy

At a glance, the run down to the first corner offers the only passing opportunity of the lap, as long as the following driver can get a sufficient tow and then do a better job under braking. But the drivers reckon that the low-speed nature of the circuit means that they can have a stab at a passing manoeuvre at numerous points around the lap, without taking too much of a risk. What they do have to watch out for, though, is heat exhaustion, as this land-locked country can be sweltering at the time of its Grand Prix slot in August, with huge electrical storms occasionally bursting overhead.

In the race's short history, the Hungaroring has been the scene of Nigel Mansell clinching the World Championship in 1992 by finishing second behind Ayrton Senna, and Damon Hill scoring his first Grand Prix win just 12 months later.

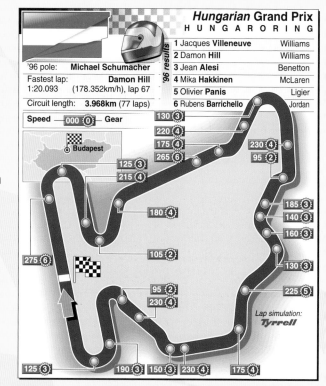

Hungarian Grand Prix
H U N G A R O R I N G

'96 results

1	Jacques **Villeneuve**	Williams
2	Damon **Hill**	Williams
3	Jean **Alesi**	Benetton
4	Mika **Hakkinen**	McLaren
5	Olivier **Panis**	Ligier
6	Rubens **Barrichello**	Jordan

'96 pole: **Michael Schumacher**
Fastest lap: **Damon Hill**
1:20.093 (178.352km/h), lap 67
Circuit length: **3.968km** (77 laps)

Speed ⎯ 000 **0** ⎯ Gear

Budapest

Lap simulation:
Tyrrell

GOING FOR GOLD: Jacques Villeneuve blasts back out of the pits en route to victory in 1996

SPA-FRANCORCHAMPS

ROUND 12, 24 AUGUST 1997

Spa-Francorchamps is the greatest racing circuit in the world. No question about it. It has a number of the leading corners, too, as it ducks and dives through the trees. But, nowhere is more exhilarating than the almost sheer uphill, Eau Rouge twister.

WHAT A VIEW! Spa offers amazing spectating opportunities. This is looking down towards Pouhon from below the Rivage hairpin

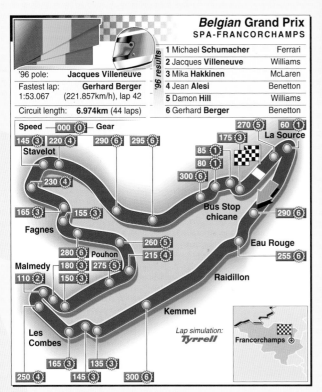

Belgian Grand Prix
SPA-FRANCORCHAMPS

'96 results

1	Michael **Schumacher**	Ferrari
2	Jacques **Villeneuve**	Williams
3	Mika **Hakkinen**	McLaren
4	Jean **Alesi**	Benetton
5	Damon **Hill**	Williams
6	Gerhard **Berger**	Benetton

'96 pole:	**Jacques Villeneuve**
Fastest lap:	**Gerhard Berger**
1:53.067	(221.857km/h), lap 42
Circuit length:	**6.974km** (44 laps)

Speed 000 Gear

Lap simulation: **Tyrrell**

Francorchamps

La Source
Stavelot
Bus Stop chicane
Eau Rouge
Fagnes
Pouhon
Malmedy
Raidillon
Kemmel
Les Combes

Unhappy alternatives

For all this eulogy about the glories of Spa, the circuit hasn't always been the home of the Belgian GP. Belgium is a country bisected by heritage, and Belgians are either Flemish from the low, coastal end of the country, or French-speaking Walloons from the end that contains Spa. Therein lay the problem. Thus the race was given to the Flemish in the early 1970s, when it was twice held at the dreadful Nivelles circuit near Brussels and then more frequently at Zolder, north-west of Liege. To compound people's misery, Zolder claimed the life of Gilles Villeneuve in 1982.

After that, the Grand Prix returned to Spa in 1983 and has been there ever since, much to everyone's delight. In its modern incarnation, the track plunges down from the La Source hairpin, just after the start, to Eau Rouge then rockets up the long hill to the esses at Les Combes, where it cuts away from the old course and dips down to the Rivage hairpin, before diving down to the double-apex left at Pouhon. After the Fagnes sweepers, it rejoins the old course and the track climbs up through the flat-out left at Blanchimont, then into the slow Bus Stop chicane.

Memorable races include Ayrton Senna lapping as fast on slicks in the rain as most of the front-runners could manage on treaded tyres in 1992, and Michael Schumacher's first win there in 1993.

Following Senna's death at Imola in 1994, Eau Rouge was considered too dangerous and it was modified, made less severe. Fortunately, sense has prevailed and drivers have accepted that there has to be some danger in racing or it would be boring, consequently the corner has been reinstated. Stand there and you will never want to watch from anywhere else again.

Amazingly, even the current circuit isn't a patch on the original Spa-Francorchamps. That used to be almost twice the length as it dived into the next valley towards Malmedy before rejoining the current track on the climb up from Stavelot. It was frighteningly fast, and there was nothing to stop an errant car from taking to the trees along its edge, or the fields if the drivers were lucky. Sadly, it claimed more than its share of fatalities, including two British drivers, Chris Bristow and Alan Stacey in the 1960 Belgian GP. Jim Clark didn't mind admitting that he loathed the place, even though he won there four times in the early 1960s.

To make matters even more risky, the weather in the Ardennes hills is notoriously fickle, and there would frequently be rain at one end of the track while it was bone dry at the other.

MONZA

ROUND 13, 7 SEPTEMBER 1997

No circuit has a spirit like Monza. Look at the unused banked corners and you're looking at another age. Yet, there's more to this parkland track than the ghosts of its past, for it's still fast and the racing is always furious there, just like the *tifosi* when the Ferraris fail to win.

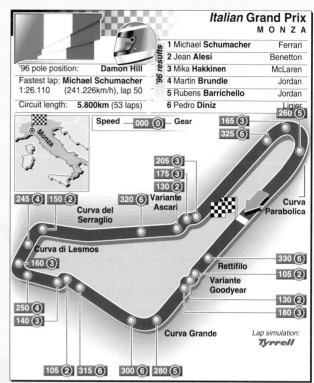

Italian Grand Prix
M O N Z A

	'96 results	
1	Michael **Schumacher**	Ferrari
2	Jean **Alesi**	Benetton
3	Mika **Hakkinen**	McLaren
4	Martin **Brundle**	Jordan
5	Rubens **Barrichello**	Jordan
6	Pedro **Diniz**	Ligier

'96 pole position: **Damon Hill**
Fastest lap: **Michael Schumacher**
1:26.110 (241.226km/h), lap 50
Circuit length: **5.800km** (53 laps)

Speed [000] [0] — Gear

Curva del Serraglio
Variante Ascari
Curva Parabolica
Curva di Lesmos
Rettifilo
Variante Goodyear
Curva Grande

Lap simulation: *Tyrrell*

To understand the *tifosi*, the Italian fans, is to understand Monza and its long, long history. Their passion for motor racing, for Formula One and for Ferrari in particular is all-consuming.

The track itself is much changed from the shape in which it was built back in 1922 in a park near Milan, when it offered both a road course and a banked oval, and many combinations of the various parts. But the basic shape of the current track is not dissimilar to the one used from the outset, except for the insertion of chicanes in 1972 to check the rocketing speed of the cars. The first of these chicanes is reached on the long run to the first "proper" corner, the right-hand Curva Grande. Even so, the Formula One cars still take this corner in fifth gear at around 175mph. Without the chicane and a full run down from the corner on to the main straight, the mind boggles at what speeds would be seen before the bend. Then, there's a straight up to the Lesmo, but in 1976 a chicane was inserted, called the Curva della Roggia, again to slow the cars. However, even with this, the two Lesmo bends are exciting enough to keep a driver's adrenaline pumping.

These right-handers were made tighter in 1994 as part of the post-Senna safety campaign. Then the cars fire off down a straight, going under the old banked circuit and into the Variante Ascari, the relatively fast third chicane inserted where a wicked left-hander used to lurk. Next up is a straight before the final corner, the famed Parabolica which catapults the cars back on to the main straight and the completion of the lap. On the first lap in 1990, Derek Warwick had something break on his Lotus and he came flying out of this corner upside down. He then brushed himself off, ran down the pit lane, got in the team's spare car and went out to take part in the restart. Brave man!

Still flying

Despite all the changes, the lap record is still just under 150mph. Pre-change, whole Grands Prix at Monza were run at that pace, with the fastest ever being in 1971, when Peter Gethin won at a race average of 150.755mph. That was also the closest Grand Prix finish of all time as his BRM was just 0.01 seconds ahead of Ronnie Peterson, with the next three cars home separated by just 0.61 seconds, after the greatest ever example of drivers hunting in a slipstreaming pack.

FAST CORNERS, WILD CROWDS: Chicanes aside, the drivers love Monza, and the *tifosi* pack out every grandstand seat

A1-RING

ROUND 14, 21 SEPTEMBER 1997

The A1-Ring is built on the site of the fabled Osterreichring and includes much of the old circuit's layout. But, sadly, not enough to keep its long, open corners. Being on the side of a hill, though, viewing is excellent.

Austrian Grand Prix
A1-RING

The Austrian Grand Prix was last staged in August 1987 on the Österreichring, located 6km west of Knittelfeld. The track has since been extensively modified and re-named

'87 Fastest lap:	Nigel Mansell
1:28.318	(242.207km/h), lap 31
Circuit length:	4.3kms

'87 results		
1	Nigel **Mansell**	Williams Honda
2	Nelson **Piquet**	Williams Honda
3	Teo **Fabi**	Benetton Ford
4	Thierry **Boutsen**	Benetton Ford
5	Ayrton **Senna**	Lotus Honda
6	Alain **Prost**	McLaren TAG Porsche

Lap times are expected to be around 1m 13s. In 91 laps of testing on, September 12, Jacques Villeneuve set a best time of 1:13.19

The return of an Austrian Grand Prix to the Formula One calendar for the first time since 1987 is exciting news not only for Austria's race fans who were brought up on a diet of local heroes such as Jochen Rindt, Niki Lauda and Gerhard Berger, but also for those who can remember the 1970s, when the race had a habit of producing first-time winners, with Vittorio Brambilla, John Watson and Alan Jones doing so in consecutive years between 1975 and 1977.

However, to everyone's disappointment, the Grand Prix will be held at the A1-Ring, a track built over the mighty Osterreichring in the rolling hills of the Styrian region. It includes some of the corners, but has lost much of the character of one of the most popular and fast circuits.

The track climbs from the grid up and over a brow to the first corner, but this comes earlier on the A1-Ring, the right-hander some 200 metres before the old Hella Licht chicane. Then there's a long climb to the Remus Kurve, now a hairpin with a steeply climbing entry. Coming out, the drivers blast up to sixth gear as they descend to the Gosser Kurve, a third gear double-apex right-hander. The track then doubles across the face of the slope for a pair of left-handers which take the track back behind the pits and fire the cars up the hill towards the final corner: the Rindt Kurve. This is now a testing right-hander followed by a tighter right which leads on to the start/finish straight.

No major races have been held yet on the A1-Ring, but the circuit certainly doesn't flow like its predecessor. And it's proved very slippery, particularly at the first corner, which should make matters interesting.

Cash, crashes and stars

It has taken the people behind the A1-Ring years of campaigning to land the financial backing required to modernize the circuit to a point where it could host a Grand Prix again. Fittingly, this second generation of Austrian Grands Prix is kicking off just as Austria's next rising star, Alexander Wurz, is approaching readiness for Formula One.

Notable races in the history of the Austrian Grand Prix include the wild events of 1975 when a deluge turned the race into a lottery. The race was stopped early with the unfancied Brambilla heading the field. So happy was he at seeing the chequered flag that he got over-excited on the slowing down lap and crashed his car. The 1982 race saw Elio de Angelis pushed all the way to the line by a fast-closing Keke Rosberg, holding on to win by 0.05 seconds, the third smallest margin ever.

ALPINE GLORY: David Coulthard found no time to admire the scenery when he tried out the A1-Ring in September 1996

 THE TRACKS

NURBURGRING

ROUND 15, 28 SEPTEMBER 1997

Germany is having two Grands Prix this year. One, at Hockenheim in July, will be the German GP. The other, at the Nurburgring in September, will be the Luxembourg GP, providing an extra sell-out for the Formula One moguls.

Like the various circuits that have hosted the European Grand Prix, the Nurburgring gives a double treat to German fans, this time under the new title of the Luxembourg Grand Prix. And like the San Marino Grand Prix – hosted outside its national boundaries at neighbouring Italy's Imola circuit – it's only a short drive from Luxembourg to the Nurburgring.

The Nurburgring hosted Germany's annual showpiece event 22 times between 1951 and 1976, then Niki Lauda was nearly killed there and it was decided that the magnificent, 14-mile Nordschleife circuit at the Nurburgring was too dangerous and the Grand Prix was moved to the purpose-built Hockenheim circuit.

A new circuit was built around the old pits area, without a single echo of the characteristics of the old Nordschleife. There are no blind brows through the trees or steeply banked corners. Instead the circuit is open and surrounded by gravel traps and grandstands. Yet, for all that and the inevitable criticism from those who hanker after the

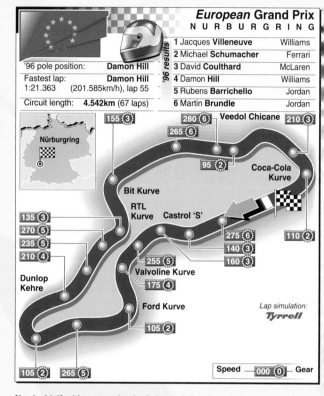

European **Grand Prix**
N U R B U R G R I N G

'96 results:
1 Jacques **Villeneuve** Williams
2 Michael **Schumacher** Ferrari
3 David **Coulthard** McLaren
4 Damon **Hill** Williams
5 Rubens **Barrichello** Jordan
6 Martin **Brundle** Jordan

'96 pole position: **Damon Hill**
Fastest lap: **Damon Hill**
1:21.363 (201.585km/h), lap 55
Circuit length: **4.542km** (67 laps)

Lap simulation: *Tyrrell*

Speed 000 0 Gear

Nordschleife, it's not such a bad circuit. It has hosted some great races since it staged the European Grand Prix in 1984: the German Grand Prix in 1985 and the European Grand Prix in 1995 and 1996.

A lap starts with a corner that never fails to entertain. It's a right-hander approached in sixth gear at around 170mph and drivers need to haul their cars down to 90mph in third to get around it. Many fail, especially on the first lap and end up in the massive gravel trap, out of which some are able to emerge providing they've kept their foot in and managed to avoid getting bogged down.

It's downhill from here through a left, a tighter right and all the way down to a second-gear hairpin. Then, going uphill, accelerating hard, there's a left-right ess and then, at the crest, the Sachskurve. This is the third-gear left-hander, out of which Damon Hill crashed in 1995, to effectively hand the title to Michael Schumacher, much to the delight of the locals.

Then the track dips downhill again through the right-hand Bitkurve, a sixth gear kink and then up again to the tight Veedol chicane where Schumacher showed his skills in passing Jean Alesi's Ferrari in that same race. Finally, there's the second gear last corner on to the main straight, out of which drivers look to get into a position to slingshot past the car ahead to make a move into the first corner.

LUXEMBOURG'S RACE: But a German crowd which will be split this year between supporting Michael Schumacher and Heinz-Harald Frentzen

120

SUZUKA

ROUND 16, 12 OCTOBER 1997

The drivers all love Suzuka. It's one of the few tracks they can really get their teeth stuck into, with the awesome 130R bend one of the fastest in the world. And the Japanese crowd is fanatical about anything that moves.

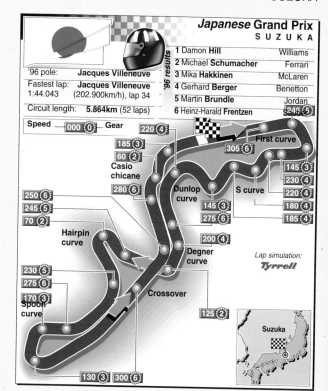

Japanese Grand Prix
SUZUKA

'96 pole: **Jacques Villeneuve**
Fastest lap: **Jacques Villeneuve**
1:44.043 (202.900km/h), lap 34
Circuit length: **5.864km** (52 laps)

'96 results:
1 Damon **Hill**	Williams
2 Michael **Schumacher**	Ferrari
3 Mika **Hakkinen**	McLaren
4 Gerhard **Berger**	Benetton
5 Martin **Brundle**	Jordan
6 Heinz-Harald **Frentzen**	Sauber

Speed 000 (0) Gear

First curve
Casio chicane
Dunlop curve
S curve
Hairpin curve
Degner curve
Spoon curve
Crossover

Lap simulation: **Tyrrell**

Suzuka

It was not until 1976 that the first Japanese Grand Prix was run and it only became a regular event after 1987, the third year it was held. This is surprising given Japan's enormous involvement in the automotive world, and the participation of the Honda Formula One team since the 1960s.

That first race was held at the Fuji Speedway at the foot of the sacred Mount Fuji volcano. Mario Andretti splashed through the rain to win that first Grand Prix, with James Hunt's third place enough to give him the world title after rival Niki Lauda pulled into the pits, refusing to race on because of the conditions. A year later, Gilles Villeneuve's Ferrari somersaulted over a fence and killed two people.

When the Japanese Grand Prix re-emerged, it was held at Suzuka, where it has remained, resisting the claim from the TI Circuit. In fact, the TI Circuit did get to hold the Pacific Grand Prix in 1994. Traditionally the last or penultimate race of the season, the Japanese Grand Prix has seen more than its share of title shoot-outs, including two between Ayrton Senna and Alain Prost in 1989 and 1990 that saw them collide on both occasions, with Prost claiming the first title as a result and Senna the second.

The enigmatic one

Suzuka is a fast and very technical circuit to race on. It really requires endless testing to learn its many intricacies. And it's clear that the drivers such as Eddie Irvine, Mika Salo and Jacques Villeneuve who knew it well from their careers in Japan before reaching Formula One have an advantage there.

From the grid, the track slopes down to the first corner, a long right-hander that sends drivers climbing back in the direction they came from in a series of esses. A fourth-gear left-hander is next, with the track dropping down to Degner Curve, a right-hander that takes the track under a bridge, with a slight kink into the hairpin, a tight left. Then it's downhill again to the Spoon curve, a long left-hander that is crucial to take correctly because it opens out on to the fastest section of the track. Half way up the straight to the final chicane comes 130R, the fastest corner on the track, taken in sixth gear at around 155mph. The final corner is the chicane at which Gerhard Berger almost collected Damon Hill on the third lap of last year's Japanese Grand Prix. So, it's tight and offers little space to avoid those demon outbreaking manoeuvres, where the driver gets it all wrong and overshoots. Then, kamikaze attacks avoided, the track bends right on to the start/finish straight.

CRUCIAL GETAWAY: Damon Hill blasts into the lead on the run to the first corner as title rival Jacques Villeneuve is swamped by the pack

ESTORIL

ROUND 17, 26 OCTOBER 1997

Grand Prix drivers know Estoril better than any other circuit, because the Portuguese track is their home from home in the winter, chosen as a test venue for its mix of fast and slow corners and its generally clement weather.

Thus, when they return there for the Grand Prix at the close of the season, they find few surprises and concentrate on going for a time in qualifying rather than having to develop their cars from scratch.

Estoril has had a Grand Prix since 1984, returning Portugal to the Formula One map for the first time since holding three Grands Prix between 1958 and 1960 in Oporto and at Monsanto, and it has provided famous races such as the one run in a deluge in 1985 when Ayrton Senna scored his first win, and the one in 1990 when Nigel Mansell and Alain Prost almost clashed going in to the first corner.

The circuit is a favourite of the drivers. At least it was before they modified it in 1994 with the insertion of crazily tight chicane two-thirds of the way around the lap.

Going down to the first corner, drivers can see little of what lies ahead as there's an earth bank on the inside of the 90-degree right-hander. All the same, they take it in fifth gear at close to 130mph, knowing that if

they get it wrong, there's a huge gravel trap to collect them. As the track dips down to the second corner, drivers are confronted by a totally different prospect: no run-off whatsoever, just a crash barrier.

Down into the first hairpin drivers have to select second before powering up to the second hairpin, this time a left-hander that feeds on to the back straight that runs along the back of the paddock before sloping down to another tightish corner. Up over a crest, the track then feeds down into Curva 7, an awkwardly cambered right-hander that immediately takes the track uphill again.

Next is the modified part of the track, the climb to a fast right-hander being truncated with the track jinking right half-way up the climb and then filtering into an extraordinarily tight uphill left-hand chicane. It's first gear and single-file. And in its short life there have been some crazy incidents here, such as last year when McLarens Mika Hakkinen crunched into the back of team-mate David Coulthard, spinning him off the track. Hard on the power, the drivers pour their cars through the previously rapid right-hander and pitch into the penultimate corner.

The last corner, Parabolica, is a long, long right-hander that feeds onto the main straight. No-one ever overtakes here. Except Jacques Villeneuve last year, when he went around the outside of Michael Schumacher. To get past requires help from the driver on the inside, otherwise the cars could touch wheels and go into orbit. It's essential to get a good exit speed, as the straight that follows is very long and, by the time the drivers consider braking again for the first corner, the best overtaking spot, most of them will be travelling at speeds close to 190mph.

Portuguese Grand Prix
E S T O R I L

'96 results

1	Jacques **Villeneuve**	Williams
2	Damon **Hill**	Williams
3	Michael **Schumacher**	Ferrari
4	Jean **Alesi**	Benetton
5	Eddie **Irvine**	Ferrari
6	Gerhard **Berger**	Benetton

'96 pole position: **Damon Hill**
Fastest lap: **Jacques Villeneuve**
1:22.873 (189.398km/h), lap 37
Circuit length: **4.360km** (70 laps)

Speed — 000 **0** — Gear

Curva Do Tanque
Parabolica
Esses
Parabolica Interior
Curva 7
Curva 3
Curva 2
VIP
Curva 1

75 2 · 200 3 · 130 3
175 3
190 3
100 2
50 1
260 5
245 5
115 2
260 5
235 5
190 3
205 5
90 2
300 6
220 5
110 3
275 6

Lap simulation: *Tyrrell*

Estoril

A TIGHT RIGHT: Jean Alesi threads his Benetton out of the tight chicane and up the hill to Curva do Tanque in the 1996 Portuguese Grand Prix

FORMULA ONE RECORDS

Who won the most Grands Prix? Was Senna more successful than Fangio? Did Mansell qualify on pole position more than Stewart? Is Ferrari still the team with the most Grand Prix wins? All these questions and many more can be answered by these easy-to-use Formula One statistics.

Most Grands Prix starts

DRIVERS

256	Riccardo Patrese (ITA)	147	Derek Warwick (GBR)
208	Andrea de Cesaris (ITA)	146	Carlos Reutemann (ARG)
204	Nelson Piquet (BRA)	144	Emerson Fittipaldi (BRA)
199	Alain Prost (FRA)	135	Jean-Pierre Jarier (FRA)
198	Gerhard Berger (AUT)	132	Eddie Cheever (USA)
194	Michele Alboreto (ITA)		Clay Regazzoni (SUI)
187	Nigel Mansell (GBR)	128	Mario Andretti (USA)
176	Graham Hill (GBR)	126	Jack Brabham (AUS)
175	Jacques Laffite (FRA)	123	Ronnie Peterson (SWE)
171	Niki Lauda (AUT)	120	Jean Alesi (FRA)
163	Thierry Boutsen (BEL)	119	Pierluigi Martini (ITA)
161	Ayrton Senna (BRA)	116	Jacky Ickx (BEL)
158	Martin Brundle (GBR)		Alan Jones (AUS)
152	John Watson (GBR)	114	Keke Rosberg (FIN)
149	Rene Arnoux (FRA)		Patrick Tambay (FRA)

CONSTRUCTORS

572	Ferrari	364	Williams	197	BRM
490	Lotus	328	Ligier/Prost	190	Minardi
445	McLaren	288	Footwork	132	Osella
394	Brabham	236	Benetton	129	Cooper
387	Tyrrell	230	March	126	Larrousse

Most Grand Prix starts without a win

208	Andrea de Cesaris (ITA)	119	Pierluigi Martini (ITA)
158	Martin Brundle (GBR)	109	Philippe Alliot (FRA)
147	Derek Warwick (GBR)	97	Chris Amon (NZL)
135	Jean-Pierre Jarier (FRA)	93	Ivan Capelli (ITA)
132	Eddie Cheever (USA)	84	Jonathan Palmer (GBR)

Most wins

DRIVERS

51	Alain Prost (FRA)		Alan Jones (AUS)
41	Ayrton Senna (BRA)		Carlos Reutemann (ARG)
31	Nigel Mansell (GBR)	10	James Hunt (GBR)
27	Jackie Stewart (GBR)		Ronnie Peterson (SWE)
25	Jim Clark (GBR)		Jody Scheckter (ZA)
	Niki Lauda (AUT)	9	Gerhard Berger (AUT)
24	Juan Manuel Fangio (ARG)	8	Denny Hulme (NZL)
23	Nelson Piquet (BRA)		Jacky Ickx (BEL)
22	Michael Schumacher (GER)	7	Rene Arnoux (FRA)
21	Damon Hill (GBR)	6	Tony Brooks (GBR)
16	Stirling Moss (GBR)		Jacques Laffite (FRA)
14	Jack Brabham (AUS)		Riccardo Patrese (FRA)
	Emerson Fittipaldi (BRA)		Jochen Rindt (AUT)
	Graham Hill (GBR)		John Surtees (GBR)
13	Alberto Ascari (ITA)		Gilles Villeneuve (CDN)
12	Mario Andretti (USA)		

CONSTRUCTORS

108	Ferrari	16	Cooper	3	March
105	McLaren	15	Renault		Wolf
96	Williams	10	Alfa Romeo	2	Honda
79	Lotus	9	Ligier	1	Eagle
35	Brabham		Maserati		Hesketh
26	Benetton		Matra		Penske
23	Tyrrell		Mercedes		Porsche
17	BRM		Vanwall		Shadow

THE MOST SUCCESSFUL: Alain Prost scored not only 51 Grand Prix wins but four World Championships

Most wins (in one season)

DRIVERS

9	Nigel Mansell (GBR) 1992		Ayrton Senna (BRA) 1991
	Michael Schumacher (GBR) 1995	6	Mario Andretti (USA) 1978
			Alberto Ascari (ITA) 1952
8	Damon Hill (GBR) 1996		Jim Clark (GBR) 1965
	Ayrton Senna (BRA) 1988		Juan Manuel Fangio (ARG) 1954
	Michael Schumacher (GER) 1994		Damon Hill (GBR) 1994
7	Jim Clark (GBR) 1963		James Hunt (GBR) 1976
	Alain Prost (FRA) 1984		Nigel Mansell (GBR) 1987
	Alain Prost (FRA) 1988		Ayrton Senna (BRA) 1989
	Alain Prost (FRA) 1993		Ayrton Senna (BRA) 1990

CONSTRUCTORS

15	McLaren 1988	7	Ferrari 1952		Ferrari 1979
12	McLaren 1984		Ferrari 1953		Ferrari 1990
	Williams 1996		Lotus 1963		Lotus 1965
11	Benetton 1995		Lotus 1973		Lotus 1970
10	McLaren 1989		Tyrrell 1971		Matra 1969
	Williams 1992		Williams 1991		McLaren 1976
	Williams 1993		Williams 1994		McLaren 1985
9	Williams 1986	6	Alfa Romeo 1950		McLaren 1990
	Williams 1987		Alfa Romeo 1951		Vanwall 1958
8	Benetton 1994		Cooper 1960		Williams 1980
	Lotus 1978		Ferrari 1975		
	McLaren 1991		Ferrari 1976		

Most consecutive wins

9	Alberto Ascari (ITA) 1952/53		Damon Hill (GBR) 1995/96
			Alain Prost (FRA) 1993
5	Jack Brabham (AUS) 1960		Jochen Rindt (AUT) 1970
	Jim Clark (GBR) 1965		Michael Schumacher (GER) 1994
	Nigel Mansell (GBR) 1992		
4	Jack Brabham (AUS) 1966		Ayrton Senna (BRA) 1988
	Jim Clark (GBR) 1963		Ayrton Senna (BRA) 1991
	Juan Manuel Fangio (ARG) 1953/54		

DOUBLE CHAMP: Jim Clark was cut short in his prime in 1968

GREAT BRITON: Nigel Mansell took the honours in 1992

World Championship wins

5	Juan Manuel Fangio (ARG)	1	Mario Andretti (USA)
4	Alain Prost (FRA)		Giuseppe Farina (ITA)
3	Jack Brabham (AUS)		Mike Hawthorn (GBR)
	Niki Lauda (AUT)		Damon Hill (GBR)
	Nelson Piquet (BRA)		Phil Hill (USA)
	Ayrton Senna (BRA)		Denis Hulme (NZL)
	Jackie Stewart (GBR)		James Hunt (GBR)
2	Alberto Ascari (ITA)		Alan Jones (AUS)
	Jim Clark (GBR)		Nigel Mansell (GBR)
	Emerson Fittipaldi (BRA)		Jochen Rindt (AUT)
	Graham Hill (GBR)		Keke Rosberg (FIN)
	Michael Schumacher (GER)		Jody Scheckter (ZA)
			John Surtees (GBR)

Constructors Cup wins

8	Ferrari	2	Brabham		Matra
	Williams		Cooper		Tyrrell
7	Lotus	1	Benetton		Vanwall
	McLaren		BRM		

Most pole positions (total)

DRIVERS

65	Ayrton Senna (BRA)	17	Jackie Stewart (GBR)
33	Jim Clark (GBR)	16	Stirling Moss (GBR)
	Alain Prost (FRA)	14	Alberto Ascari (ITA)
32	Nigel Mansell (GBR)		James Hunt (GBR)
28	Juan Manuel Fangio (ARG)		Ronnie Peterson (SWE)
24	Niki Lauda (AUT)		Michael Schumacher (GER)
	Nelson Piquet (BRA)	13	Jack Brabham (AUS)
20	Damon Hill (GBR)		Graham Hill (GBR)
18	Mario Andretti (USA)		Jacky Ickx (BEL)
	Rene Arnoux (FRA)	11	Gerhard Berger (AUT)

CONSTRUCTORS

118	Ferrari	13	Benetton	7	Vanwall
107	Lotus	12	Alfa Romeo	5	March
99	Williams	11	BRM	4	Matra
79	McLaren		Cooper	3	Shadow
39	Brabham	10	Maserati	2	Lancia
31	Renault	9	Ligier	1	Jordan
14	Tyrrell	8	Mercedes		

POLE KING: Ayrton Senna secured a record 65 pole positions

Most fastest laps

DRIVERS

41	Alain Prost (FRA)		Damon Hill (GBR)
30	Nigel Mansell (GBR)		Ayrton Senna (BRA)
28	Jim Clark (GBR)	15	Clay Regazzoni (SUI)
25	Niki Lauda (AUT)		Jackie Stewart (GBR)
	Michael Schumacher (GER)	14	Jacky Ickx (BEL)
23	Juan Manuel Fangio (ARG)	13	Alan Jones (AUS)
	Nelson Piquet (BRA)		Riccardo Patrese (ITA)
20	Stirling Moss (GBR)	12	Rene Arnoux (FRA)
19	Gerhard Berger (AUT)	11	Alberto Ascari (ITA)
			John Surtees (GBR)

CONSTRUCTORS

124	Ferrari	20	Tyrrell	12	Matra
102	Williams	18	Renault	11	Ligier
71	Lotus	15	BRM	9	Mercedes
69	McLaren		Maserati	7	March
40	Brabham	14	Alfa Romeo	6	Vanwall
32	Benetton	13	Cooper		

Most pole positions (in one season)

DRIVERS

14	Nigel Mansell (GBR) 1992		Nelson Piquet (BRA) 1984
13	Alain Prost (FRA) 1993	8	Mario Andretti (USA) 1978
	Ayrton Senna (BRA) 1988		James Hunt (GBR) 1976
	Ayrton Senna (BRA) 1989		Nigel Mansell (GBR) 1987
10	Ayrton Senna (BRA) 1990		Ayrton Senna (BRA) 1986
9	Damon Hill (GBR) 1996		Ayrton Senna (BRA) 1991
	Niki Lauda (AUT) 1974	7	Mario Andretti (USA) 1977
	Niki Lauda (AUT) 1975		Jim Clark (GBR) 1963
	Ronnie Peterson (SWE) 1973		Ayrton Senna (BRA) 1985

CONSTRUCTORS

15	McLaren 1988		McLaren 1990		Lotus 1973
	McLaren 1989		Williams 1987		McLaren 1991
	Williams 1992		Williams 1995		Renault 1982
	Williams 1993		Williams 1996	9	Brabham 1984
12	Lotus 1978	10	Ferrari 1974		Ferrari 1975

Most points

DRIVERS

798.5	Alain Prost (FRA)	289	Graham Hill (GBR)
614	Ayrton Senna (BRA)	281	Emerson Fittipaldi (BRA)
485.5	Nelson Piquet (BRA)		Riccardo Patrese (ITA)
482	Nigel Mansell (GBR)	277.5	Juan Manuel Fangio (ARG)
420.5	Niki Lauda (AUT)	274	Jim Clark (GBR)
370	Michael Schumacher (GER)	261	Jack Brabham (AUS)
367	Gerhard Berger (AUT)	255	Jody Scheckter (ZA)
360	Jackie Stewart (GBR)	248	Denny Hulme (NZL)
326	Damon Hill (GBR)	228	Jacques Laffite (FRA)
310	Carlos Reutemann (ARG)	212	Clay Regazzoni (SUI)

CONSTRUCTORS

2002.5	McLaren	439	BRM	88	Jordan
1999.5	Ferrari	395	Ligier/Prost	79	Wolf
1809.5	Williams	333	Cooper	67.5	Shadow
1352	Lotus	312	Renault	57	Vanwall
854	Brabham	171.5	March	54	Sauber
741.5	Benetton	155	Matra		
615	Tyrrell	141	Footwork		

HILL SENIOR: Graham Hill was twice World Champion

1997 Formula One Grand Prix Calendar

DATE	GRAND PRIX	TRACK	1ST	2ND	3RD	4TH	5TH	6TH	POLE
Mar 9	Australian GP	Melbourne	Coulthard	M Schumacher	Hakkinen	Berger	Panis	Larini	Villeneuve
Mar 30	Brazilian GP	Interlagos	Villeneuve	Berger	Panis	Hakkinen	M Schumacher	Alesi	Villeneuve
Apr 13	Argentinian GP	Buenos Aires							
Apr 27	San Marino GP	Imola							
May 11	Monaco GP	Monaco							
May 25	Spanish GP	Barcelona							
June 15	Canadian GP	Montreal							
June 29	French GP	Magny-Cours							
July 13	British GP	Silverstone							
July 27	German GP	Hockenheim							
Aug 10	Hungarian GP	Hungaroring							
Aug 24	Belgian GP	Spa							
Sept 7	Italian GP	Monza							
Sept 21	Austrian GP	A1-Ring							
Sept 28	Luxembourg GP	Nurburgring							
Oct 12	Japanese GP	Suzuka							
Oct 26	Portuguese GP	Estoril							

Final World Drivers' Championship Standings 1997

POSITION	DRIVER	NATIONALITY	TEAM	POLES	PTS
1					
2					
3					
4					
5					
6					
7					
8					
9					
10					
11					
12					
13					
14					
15					
16					
17					
18					
19					
20					

Final Constructors' Championship Standings 1997

POSITION	TEAM	POINTS
1		
2		
3		
4		
5		
6		
7		
8		
9		
10		

TAKING THE PRESSURE: Hill makes a grab for Villeneuve

NO EXCUSES ACCEPTED: Benetton's heavy-hitters watch the progress of their men, Alesi and Berger, from the pitwall

Picture Credits

The publishers would like to thank the following sources for their kind permission to reproduce the photographs in this book.

Allsport: Graham Chadwick 57; Michael Cooper 27, 95, 104, 105, 106, 107; Vincent Kalut 43, Clive Mason 56; Mike Powell 84; Ben Radford 16, 25, 41br, 45, 69, 113, 114,116; Pascal Rondeau 3, 9, 15, 31, 39, 54, 61, 63, 71, 74, 83, 88, 89, 109, 111, 120, 121, 124tr, 128; Vandystadt/Vincent Kalut 64, 112, Jean-Marc Loubat 17, Alain Patrice 52, 80, 103, 122; Anton Want 23; **Allsport Historical Collection:** Hulton Getty 125bl; MSI 124bl; **Benetton Renault:** 47, 48, 49. **Colorsport:** Cesare Galimberti 82, Olympia 92. **Empics Sports Photo Agency:** 76; Steve Etherington 4tr, 10tr, 24, 41tl, 81, 86, 87; Claire Mackintosh 20, 67; John Marsh 12, 14, 18, 19, 29, 32, 44, 77. **F1 Pictures:** 100. **LAT Photographic:** 7. **Minardi Formula One:** 60. **Sporting Pictures:** 21, 28, 42, 66, 68, 70, 73, 75, 79, 85, 90, 96, 108, 110, 117, 118, 123. **Sutton Motorsport Images:** 1, 2, 4, 5tr, 5bl, 10b, 11, 22, 26, 40, 46, 50, 53, 55, 78, 93, 94, 98, 101, 115, 125tr, 127; Alezra 97; Amaduzzi 119; Galeron 91, 99; Lawerence 72; Tsuboi 58, 59.

Every effort has been made to acknowledge correctly and contact the source and/or copyright holder of each picture, and Carlton Books Limited apologises for any unintentional errors or omissions which will be corrected in future editions of this book.

Illustrations

Illustrations on pages 34–37 and 106–22 © Russell Lewis, other illustrations are reproduced by permission of Geoff Fowler.